FALL
=OF AN=
ARROW

First edition published in 1978 by Canada's Wings

Published in 2001 by
Stoddart Publishing Co. Limited
895 Don Mills Road
400-2 Park Centre
Toronto, Canada
M3C 1W3
Tel. (416) 445-3333
Fax (416) 445-5967

Fifth printing January 2001

Distributed in Canada by:
General Distribution Services Limited
325 Humber College Blvd., Toronto, Canada M9W 7C3
Tel. (416) 213-1919 Fax (416) 213-1917
Email cservice@genpub.com

Distributed in the United States by:
General Distribution Services Inc.
PMB 128, 4500 Witmer Industrial Estates
Niagara Falls, New York 14305-1386
Toll-free tel. 1-800-805-1083 Toll-free fax 1-800-481-6207
Email gdsinc@genpub.com

Canadian Cataloguing in Publication Data

Peden, Murray, 1923–
Fall of an Arrow

ISBN 0-7737-5105-X

1. Avro Arrow (Turbojet fighter plane).
2. Aircraft Industry – Canada.   3. Canada – Politics and government –
1957-1963.   I. Title.

TL685.3.P43 1987   338.4'76237464'0971   C87-094252-2

U.S. Cataloging-in-Publication Data available
from the Library of Congress

Cover illustration: Peter Moseman
Cover design: Brant Cowie/Artplus

We acknowledge for their financial support of our publishing program the Canada Council, the Ontario Arts Council, and the Government of Canada through the Book Publishing Industry Development Program (BPIDP).

Printed and bound in Canada

FALL
OF AN
ARROW

MURRAY PEDEN

Contents

CHAPTER I

CHAPTER II

CHAPTER III

CHAPTER IV

CHAPTER V

Chapter 1

Just three days before the 50th anniversary of powered flight in Canada[1] the Prime Minister rose in the House of Commons in Ottawa and made a statement the effect of which was to dash the struggling Canadian military aircraft and engine industry from its proud position as temporary leader of the western world — perhaps the whole world — and relegate it, almost instantly, to the outermost boondocks of the industrial minor leagues. When the Right Honourable John George Diefenbaker announced the cancellation of the CF-105 *Arrow* on Friday, February 20th, 1959, he demolished in one brutally final stroke what another Member of Parliament publicly categorized as "the greatest single achievement in Canadian aviation history, and the greatest combined effort of design and development ever undertaken in this country".

That Member went on to say: "Not only that, I regret, and I want to put this on record again, that this government, did not have the courage to finish *(Arrow)* No. 6 and let it take the world's speed record away from the Lockheed 104. I think this is a matter which

---

1. J. A. D. McCurdy, later Lieutenant-Governor of Nova Scotia, flew the *Silver Dart* from the ice of Bras D'Or Lake in Nova Scotia on February 23rd, 1909.

will cause regret to Canadians for decades to come — that when we had reached a stage where, in a few weeks of additional development and testing, this plane could have captured the world's speed record for this country, the decision should have been made not only to stop work on the plane but to cut up the corpse and put it underground as soon as possible."

These strong comments came from a political opponent; but many Conservatives in the House, and scores of thousands more across the country, shared Liberal Paul Hellyer's indignation. The *Arrow* affair cut sharply across party lines.

John Diefenbaker had become Prime Minister through the interplay of the usual mix of political forces, coupled with an exhibition of tenacity, showmanship and ability on his own part. But able as he undoubtedly was in many ways, John Diefenbaker showed marked weakness and vacillation in the formulation and implementation of National Defence policy, and in the related aspects of foreign policy. His government's strangely skewed assessment of the *Arrow* situation, which seemed at times to reflect personality clashes and a studied hostility to the project more than the objectivity it purported to be founded upon, set in train a flood of criticism. In due course it also precipitated a series of dependent events which were to cause serious and worsening political problems, ultimately resulting in the fall of the government. The self-destruction of the Diefenbaker administration over the non-issue of nuclear warheads for *Bomarc* missiles was directly linked to the cancellation of the *Arrow*.

Like some nightmarish reversal of the standard Horatio Alger story, a reversal in which the climax saw multiplying misfortunes cascading upon the hero, the demise of the CF-105 *Arrow* produced a series of scenes that taxed credulity, even amongst the government's staunchest supporters. Having just completed the spending of over 340 million dollars of the Canadian taxpayers' money for the purpose of designing and building an interceptor aircraft to have a performance unsurpassed anywhere in the world — and having been spectacularly successful in producing an aircraft carrying those prestigious credentials — here was the Prime Minister cancelling the six-year long program at the very moment it was about to reach fruition, seemingly not fully realizing what would shortly ensue. The February 20th cancellation announcement caused the discharge that very afternoon of approximately 14,000 skilled employees at the A. V. Roe Canada Limited's plants in Malton, and the abrupt cessation of work for an estimated 15,000 other skilled tradesmen employed by the 2500 subcontractors and suppliers linked with A. V. Roe on this great project. Many of those subcontractors and suppliers, firms that had expanded to handle Avro Aircraft Ltd.'s growing requirements, were soon petitioned into bankruptcy.

As if that were not enough to have to answer for, the Minister of Defence Production, the Honourable Raymond O'Hurley, had to rise in his place on April 22nd, to correct a misstatement he had inadvertently made the previous day and acknowledge that five almost fully completed *Arrow* aircraft were in fact being dismembered by workmen with acetylene torches at that very moment. And although he announced that "the five *finished* craft have not been touched" the fact was that the government's incredible ineptitude in this phase of the affair was going to see those other five machines as well, superb machines in flying condition, torched into small pieces of industrial excreta in readiness for their consignment to a place of honour in a Hamilton junkyard.

This appalling act of vandalism, perpetrated on five finished and flyable aircraft that the Prime Minister had indicated were costing the taxpayers approximately $12,500,000 each, was regarded by many as exceeding in callousness the government's brutality in causing the immediate dismissal of all the workmen. The abrupt dismissal, though inept, had at least been unintentional. In fairness to the Prime Minister, he had relied on the fact that under the contract the government was liable for approximately three weeks' severance pay, and that there was available in the departmental estimates another $50,000,000 to cushion the impact of the cancellation and provide transitional relief for the large and highly skilled work force dependent upon the project's continuance.

But in its anxiety to end once and for all what it chose to regard only as a running financial sore, and to ensure that there would be no further buying of expensive material, either for the aircraft or for its engines, the government sent a telegram which could only be construed as ordering the immediate firing of the 14,000 Avro Aircraft and Orenda Engines workers in Malton. Mr. O'Hurley admitted frankly that he was under the impression that the men would continue to work for their ordinary period of time on notice, which was two weeks or three weeks. Manfully he stood before the House and admitted: "I was most surprised myself to hear the same evening the men were let out that afternoon. The telegram was sent with my concurrence." The unfortunate fact was that both the telegram to Avro, marked for the attention of Mr. J. L. Plant, Malton, and the telegram directed to Orenda Engines, from an official in the Department of Production, used precisely the same blunt language: "You shall cease all work immediately." The telegrams left the company absolutely no elbow room.

It would have taken Shakespearean tragedy itself to outdo the protracted demise of the CF-105 *Arrow* for over-all emotional impact, for, superimposed on the consciousness of everyone watching this painful affair was the gnawing uncertainty injected by the repetitively insistent tone of *Sputnik* I's beeper. That harbinger of revolutionary change had first startled the world on October 4th, 1957 — ironically, the very day on which the first completed *Arrow* had been towed in triumph from its hangar at Malton for a "roll-out" ceremony as a prelude to its impending ground trials.

The rapid advance of Russian space technology generally, and particularly the unexpectedly rapid strides in missile capability demonstrated by *Sputnik's* launching, was destined to be one of the several factors that sealed the fate of Canada's most advanced military aircraft, leaving Canada, after Prime Minister Diefenbaker threw in the towel, to join the many nations wholly dependent upon the United States for research, design and development in the aircraft industry.

It had been a courageous attempt to avoid just such dependence that had started the whole *Arrow* saga.

The striking success of Canada's venture into the esoteric field of supersonic flight had never been fully grasped by the majority of Canada's newsmen and commentators — experts and prophets being notoriously underrated in their own bailiwicks — hence the realization of their country's tremendous accomplishment had been slow to germinate amongst most Canadians. Only after the hasty burial of the corpse had many of them come to appreciate what had been thrown away by a nation that had hitherto been one of the most adventurously air-minded in the world.

Chapter 2

After World War II, the RCAF was engaged in a search for a new fighter capable of performing the somewhat specialized role required of an interceptor operating over the vast and sparsely populated areas of Canada. Tactical factors militated in favour of an aircraft of considerable range, preferably a twin-engined all-weather aircraft carrying both a pilot and a navigator/radar operator. Air Marshal W. A. Curtis was authorized to lead a team of RCAF specialists given the assignment of checking with aircraft manufacturers all over North America and the United Kingdom to see whether any fighter with the specifications they had in mind was nearing production, or even on the drawing board. Neither in the United States nor Britain was such an aircraft to be found.

Air Marshal Curtis recommended that an aircraft designed to meet the specifications compiled by the RCAF be built in Canada. From bitter experience in World War II he had learned what happened when a country was dependent upon other countries for its weapons. RCAF squadrons had frequently been in the unenviable position of having to accept second-grade aeroplanes that had become surplus to American or British requirements. Thus Canadian fighter squadrons had been flying anemic *Mohawks* and P-40's when better aircraft were urgently required for first line service, and were in fact being used by the countries building them. No. 6 Group, the RCAF Group in RAF Bomber Command, still had a number of squadrons flying *Halifaxes* at the end of the war despite the fact that the *Lancaster* was a better aircraft, and the more pertinent fact that Canadian factories had built some 400 *Lancasters* under licence by that time. But those aircraft had not been under the allocational control of the Canadian government. The lesson was abundantly clear: if a government expected to be able to funnel first line planes to its own squadrons, from the first years' production runs available, it had to build them itself.

Of even more importance to a country, from a long-term point of view, was the fact that by designing and building its own aircraft it automatically acquired two concomitant benefits of great value. Firstly, it got aircraft tailored specifically to its own needs in the combat role it chose to assume. Secondly, it acquired and retained the skilled work force, the technological expertise, and the sophisticated testing facilities that enabled it to keep pace with, or outdistance, its competitors or potential enemies. Building, under licence, aircraft that had been designed, tested, modified and brought into production elsewhere, is not a remotely comparable substitute. There is a critically important time factor involved in copying another country's designs. In the aircraft industry an elapsed time of six years between first drawings and first production run is probably close to the norm. So a country content to copy another's production aircraft is soon many years behind in design and testing technology. Thus the short-term "bargain" seemingly obtained by the avoidance of research and development costs is frequently the path to more and more economic and technological dependence. This was certainly not the path most thinking Canadians wanted to tread, Canada being a country which from its birth had rejected the status of "hewers of wood and drawers of water". Air Marshal Curtis' group were well aware of all the factors involved, and any recommendation W. A. Curtis made merited careful consideration.

Air Marshal Wilfred Austin Curtis was a Canadian who had

served his country well. In World War I, as a young man of 23, he had transferred from the Canadian Army to the Royal Naval Air Service in 1916. As a fighter pilot he had then won the status of "Ace", with 13 victories to his credit; and during 1917 and 1918 he won the Distinguished Service Cross twice, together with several Mentions in Despatches, before being wounded and sent home.

Between wars, apart from earning his living as a private businessman, Curtis served in the Reserves for eight years as an officer in the Toronto Scottish, later helping to organize the 110th City of Toronto RCAF Reserve Squadron.

He re-enlisted in the RCAF in September, 1939, and for a second time served his country with distinction. He held a series of senior posts, including that of Deputy Commander-in-Chief RCAF Overseas, and, later, Air Member for Air Staff and senior officer on the Permanent Joint Board of Defence between Canada and the United States. In the course of his second war's service he earned several more distinguished awards: Commander of the Order of the British Empire, Companion of the Bath, United States Legion of Merit (Commander), the Croix de Guerre with Palm, the French Legion of Honour (Chevalier) and the Commandatore dell Ordine Militare d'Italia.

In 1947 Air Marshal Curtis was named Chief of Air Staff, in which capacity his first act, typically, was to launch a thoroughgoing modernization program in the RCAF, one aspect of which was this search for a new fighter.

The recommendation of Air Marshal Curtis and his team was acted upon in due course, with the result that the highly successful CF-100[1] was designed and built in the A. V. Roe Canada Limited plants at Malton, near Toronto. This company was a holding company (which later went public) organized by Sir Roy Dobson at the behest of, and controlled by, the British Hawker-Siddeley Group. The operating subsidiaries directly concerned were Avro Aircraft Ltd. and Orenda Engines Ltd. The companies' CF-100 was widely recognized as a first class aeroplane, and in fact proved so success-

---

1. The requirement for the CF-100 was actually established before Air Marshal Curtis became Chief of Air Staff.

Above: *Air Marshal Wilfred Austin Curtis, standing with the Governor-General of Canada, His Excellency Viscount Alexander of Tunis, and Flight Lieutenant Wright, RCAF. Curtis was a most capable officer, an apt choice for the moderniser the RCAF required in the transitional period after World War II. He died in Toronto on August 7th, 1977, only a few weeks after responding to the author's letter and offering to assist in the preparation of this account of the Arrow's history.* (PUBLIC ARCHIVES OF CANADA)

Below: *This CF-100 18393 was photographed by the author in May, 1977, at the former RAF Fighter Base at Duxford, England. Notice that the wingtip pods have been detached.* (AUTHOR)

Above: *A CF-100 "Canuck" Mark IV-B 18362 of 428 "Ghost" Squadron, RCAF flying near Uplands, Ontario, on May 10th, 1955.*
(PAC PL-87684)

Left: *Another more recent view of the CF-100, the RCAF's twin engine, all-weather interceptor, 100780 of 414 (EW) Sqn. The paint scheme makes the wing pods particularly prominent in this shot.*
(CANADIAN ARMED FORCES)

Below: *A CF-100 still flying today (May, 1978). This one, 100783 of 414 (EW) Sqn., was flown to Winnipeg, site of Air Command Headquarters, to participate in the celebration of the 50th anniversary of Stevenson Field.* (A. B. PEDEN)

Avro Aircraft Ltd. made its mark in the military aircraft design field with the CF-100 "Canuck", an outstandingly successful aircraft. The power and reliability of its Orenda engines also became noteworthy.

Above left: *Prime Minister Louis St. Laurent, who succeeded Mackenzie King as head of the Liberal party in Canada. A respected and highly successful corporation lawyer, Mr. St. Laurent had been persuaded to enter the Mackenzie King Cabinet during World War II.* (PAC)

Above right: *C. D. Howe, as Minister of Munitions and Supply, speaking in the course of a victory loan campaign in Sudbury, Ontario, February 17th, 1942. Howe was an engineer and an energetic advocate of business.* (PAC C-19380)

Left: *Another view of Right Honourable C. D. Howe, as he appeared at the time of the Arrow affair.*

NO
SMOKING.

Left: *Charles A. Grinyer, who figured so prominently in the development of the Orenda Iroquois, an engine 20 years ahead of its time. This photograph was taken only a few months after the cancellation of the Arrow and Iroquois programs.*
(CHARLES A. GRINYER)

Above: *This photo gives ample indication of the massive size of the Iroquois engine.*
(Via P. J. BRENNAN)

21

Above: *The Iroquois engine in its most unusual rear-fuselage mounting on a B-47 Stratojet. This aircraft was loaned to the RCAF at no cost by the USAF specifically for the flight testing of this very powerful engine.*

(P. J. BRENNAN)

Below: *The size and complexity of the main undercarriage of the Arrow are suggested in this photo and line drawing. The undercarriage members were designed and built by Dowty of Canada Ltd., the tires and brakes by Goodyear.*

(AIR AND SPACE DIVISION, NATIONAL MUSEUM, OTTAWA)

Right: *The great vent into supersonic airc design gets underway on production line. The wo man sitting just below nose affords a bench m for judging the size of Arrow. The cockpit equipped to take a Mar Baker C.5 ejection seat.*

(CANADIAN ARMED FORC

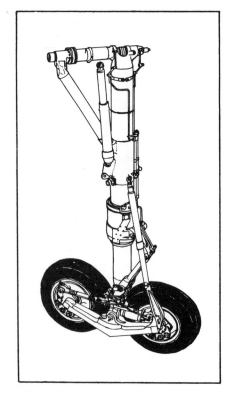

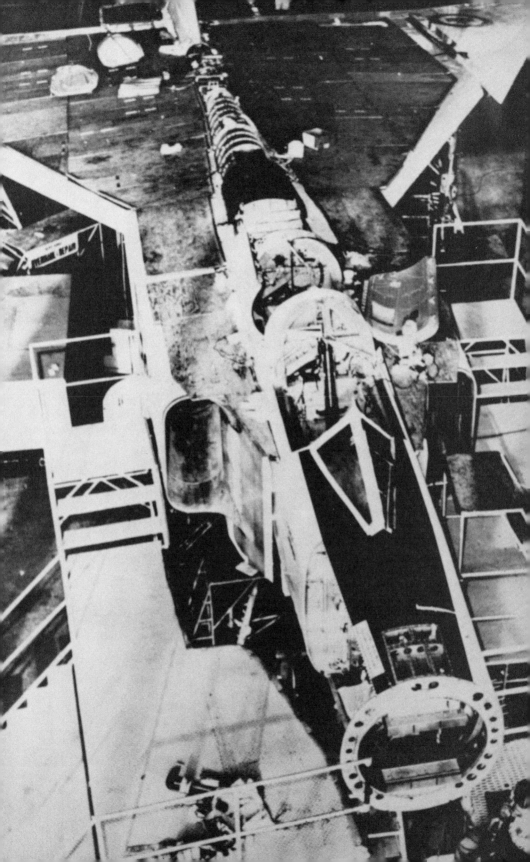

Centre fuselage assemblies under production in the Avro plant. Note the large amount of wiring to be put into place.
(Via P. J. BRENNAN)

ful in its all-weather interceptor role that some $50,000,000 worth were purchased by Belgium for the discharge of its newly assumed NATO responsibilities.

In 1951, bearing in mind the lengthy period between design and production, the RCAF began looking ahead again to the new aeroplane that would succeed the CF-100, and serious studies were initiated. Again highly ambitious and distinctive requirements were suggested, and ultimately embodied in the RCAF's "Final Report of the All-Weather Interceptor Requirements Team" which was delivered in March, 1952, to Avro Aircraft. (Another canvass of aircraft factories in all the NATO countries, particularly the American plants, had indicated that no aircraft with similar performance requirements was even being planned elsewhere.)

The new Canadian interceptor sought was to be a twin-engined, long-range all-weather machine, capable of high speeds to enable it to catch the bombers which it was anticipated would be in the Soviet inventory by the late 50's and early 60's. It would be a two-place aeroplane like the CF-100, but it would be supersonic; it was to carry a highly sophisticated fire control and weapons system, of which the most promising type then appeared to be the American Hughes MX-1179, complemented by six *Falcon* missiles.

Discussions with A. V. Roe were carried on in 1952, and in 1953 the Liberal government of Prime Minister Louis St. Laurent made the momentous decision to proceed with the development of the radically new design and the production of two prototypes. The initial appropriation approved was for $30,000,000. Unit cost on a production run was roughly estimated, on the assumption that five hundred or six hundred aircraft would be needed by the RCAF. The unit cost derived on the basis of those ball park figures appeared to be one and a half million or two million dollars per aircraft. (The CF-100, Mark V, was then being turned out at $750,000 per unit.)

Right Honourable C. D. Howe, Minister of Defence Production, made the uncharacteristic statement: ". . . we have started on a program of development that gives me the shudders, a supersonic plane and a supersonic engine . . . Before we get through it will be around $100 million. That is a program no other country has carried through successfully as yet." He was talking about development cost alone, of course, when he spoke of a total of $100 million. Obviously if he visualized the production of 600 aircraft at a cost of $2 million each, he was prepared to spend an additional $1.2 billion of the taxpayers' money, over and above any unamortized portion of the $100 million development cost. The total outlay would be spread over many years; nevertheless C. D. Howe had the jitters, and C. D. Howe was not known as a man of frugal habits where spending in the grand manner could be justified. Avro Aircraft Ltd. ignored the reports of his belated timidity and self-doubts and set about the task in hand.

The new interceptor, styled the CF-105 *Arrow*, was to be a tailless, (i.e. lacking horizontal stabilizers) high delta wing aircraft, this decision on the configuration flowing from an analysis of weight and efficiency factors. To James C. Floyd, the aero-dynamics engineer carrying over-all responsibility for the design[1], the delta wing promised the lightest wing for a low thickness to chord ratio while still providing, due to its large root chord, satisfactory thickness for fuel and undercarriage stowage. A wing area of 1200 square feet was settled on, representing in the design team's view the optimum compromise between minimum weight and maximum performance. High wing placement promised the lowest weight coupled with the easiest access to engines, armament and electronic gear.

From July, 1953 until July, 1954, a great deal of preliminary design work was carried out establishing loads, basic aerodynamic parameters and dimensions. Of these multitudinous tests and experiments the public heard next to nothing, of course, either while they were being carried out or later. The magnitude of the enterprise was never broadly understood. The contracts with the company were modified — actually, replaced with a series of separate contracts. Now several Mark I "prototypes" were planned, then a Mark II

---

1. J. C. Floyd's official title at Avro Aircraft Ltd. was Vice-President Engineering. His great strength was as a structures engineer. He had been Project Engineer for the Avro Jetliner for which he received the Wright award. Basically the aerodynamics of the *Arrow* originated in the brain of the brilliant Jim Chamberlin, a Canadian who had taken part of his education in England.

series, the latter to include a further number of test aircraft before authorization was given for the final production run.

For the Mark I *Arrow* three power plants had been considered: the Rolls Royce RB-106, the Bristol B.OL.4, and the Curtiss-Wright J-67. All three units were equipped with afterburners, but all three were also in the early development stage and had not yet run. The engine finally selected was the Rolls Royce RB-106; but in 1954 Rolls Royce decided to abandon its development. The decision was then made to switch to the Curtiss-Wright J-67 for the first prototypes of the CF-105 *Arrow* and to turn to the design of a new and more powerful engine — to be developed in the Orenda plant — for later models of the aircraft. On that decision, more anon.

The Arrow project, so much more ambitious than the work on the CF-100, required a substantial enlargement of Avro's design and support teams. Exotic techniques not required in construction of subsonic aircraft were demanded by the new problems of supersonic flight, so specialists with the requisite skills had to be recruited. E. J. Silling, an English mechanical engineer, might be taken as representative. He had had several years experience in aircraft design, prefaced by a stint during World War II as an RAF technical instructor, before starting his design career on the *Canberra,* the world's second jet bomber[1]. After emigrating to Canada he worked on the CF-100, then transferred to the *Arrow* team.

Asked about the formation of that group, Silling responded: "The design team was composed of Englishmen, Canadians, Poles and Americans. The Englishmen were in the majority, as Avro had just completed their third annual recruiting drive through the British Isles. Canadians were local men, mostly in administrative positions. The Poles were recruited in Britain, and the Americans [were] contract workers, hired by Avro from a broker. The most outstanding Englishman[2] was an absolute wizard on aerodynamics. A Cambridge don, I believe. The Poles were very good — mostly key men from the Polish aircraft industry. The most outstanding Pole

---

1. The German Arado 234B Blitz has a legitimate claim to being the first.
2. This would appear to be a reference to Jim Chamberlin.

was a mathematician whose capabilities in those days of slide rules and simple adding machines just bordered on sorcery. Among the Americans, one produced mind-boggling designs of sophisticated hydraulic components. Another worked on the drag chute, producing in the process several innovations patented by Avro . . . The head of the *Arrow* design team was an Englishman named Frost[1]. From the outset sights were set very high. At every staff meeting held to discuss some problem or decision, the opening phrase was: 'This has never been attempted before. But sometime in the future it will be done. Let us do it now' ''.

Preliminary wind tunnel work had been carried out prior to mid-1954 when the first production drawings were completed and passed to manufacturing. At this point the complex aerodynamics of supersonic flight required intensive wind tunnel work. The American National Aeronautics and Space Administration (NASA) made available some of its extensive facilities, free of charge. An assortment of additional problems and deadlines accompanied the RCAF's decision to switch from the proven Hughes fire control system and to design and install instead a completely new weapons and fire control system of even more advanced specifications. The new system, called "ASTRA", was to be developed in Canada by RCA, Honeywell Controls, and Computing Devices of Canada.

A. V. Roe Ltd. argued against this switch, which was going to produce a limited improvement in weapons system efficiency at a potentially heavy financial cost. The RCAF and its directorate of Armament Engineering were adamant; not only were they switching to ASTRA as the weapons and fire control system, they were switching to a new and undeveloped missile as well — the *Sparrow II*.

---

1. The *Arrow* Project Engineer was actually Bob Lindley, who later became Chief Engineer. John Frost was one of Avro's many innovative designers. In 1951 he had embarked upon the design and development of a flying saucer, after having studied their aerodynamic efficiency for a lengthy period. He eventually built a flying model at Avro, but encountered seemingly insurmountable control problems every time he got the craft airborne. The Canadian government gave up and withdrew its backing after spending approximately $2,000,000. The United States government persevered, and backed Frost's project to the tune of $10,000,000., but eventually shelved it, the control problem not having been satisfactorily mastered.

Chapter 3

If the Canadian public were seldom adequately informed by newsmen of the remarkable accomplishments of their aircraft industry in designing and building the supersonic *Arrow*, they were told even less about the complementary achievement of Orenda Engines Ltd. in designing and building the *Iroquois* engine. True, trade publications carried accurate articles on the progress of this magnificent power plant; but by and large the daily newspapers and the commentators missed the significance of Orenda's great success. Certainly they missed most of the hundred and one minor technological triumphs that would have given their readers, listeners and viewers some benchmarks upon which to formulate a proper appraisal. This untypical myopia could not be blamed on the tight security maintained on certain critical performance data. The trade papers, including the Company's own "Avro Canada News" and "Orenda", published a wealth of material through which the magnitude of the developments were reasonably obvious to anyone who wished to look.

By contrast, Canadian newsmen had been at pains as recently as 1953 to make the public aware that Orenda-built engines had been highly successful when installed in the American designed — but Canadair-built — *Sabre* jets being flown by the RCAF. Similarly, when the RCAF moved on to the Orenda-powered CF-100's, the excellent performance of both engine and aircraft were widely reported.

In the development of the P.S. 13 *Iroquois* engine, Canada's newsmen had at hand a gold-plated Canadian success story; yet few of them gave it more than passing mention. The story certainly seemed to warrant ample coverage. Here was a newly-formed Canadian company not only competing with the American "Big Three" in gas turbines — Pratt & Whitney, General Electric, and Curtiss-Wright — but competing so successfully as to have one of the Big Three come to Orenda in due course to negotiate a contract for the rights to build this remarkable engine under licence in the United States.

Every literate adult in Canada knew the vital part played in World War II by the famous Rolls Royce aero-engines, particularly the great *Merlins* that powered the *Spitfire*, the *Hurricane*, the *Mosquito*, the P-51 *Mustang*, and thousands of *Lancasters*. But it is doubtful that more than a handful of Canadians ever came to realize that Canada's Orenda *Iroquois* marked a greater advance over its predecessors and competitors than the *Merlin* engine had over its immediate progenitors. The full story of the *Iroquois'* development, detailing the skill and determination displayed in the conquest of its early technical problems, would require a book in itself. Here, a thumbnail sketch must suffice.

In 1951 and 1952, Orenda had tried unsuccessfully to interest the RCAF in the development of a new jet engine, this time one with approximately 12,000 pounds thrust[1]. The failure of these efforts, and the prospective development by American engine manufacturers of power plants that would be reasonably comparable, persuaded Orenda's management that they would have to embark upon a much more ambitious project in order to be competitive after the lengthy development period, particularly against the "Big Three".

---

1. The Canadair-built F-86 *Sabres*, styled the CL-13B Mk 6, were powered with the Orenda 14, which had no afterburner and delivered a maximum thrust of 7600 pounds.

Orenda's answer was Project Study 13 (P.S. 13) which it was thought would ensure the necessary lead over the competition if it could be brought off. The concept involved a radical increase in power and a marked improvement in the critical thrust-to-weight ratio. A key figure in this substantial undertaking was Charles A. Grinyer.

Charles Grinyer joined the A. V. Roe complex in Canada in April, 1952. His earlier career had included a stint in England with the Bristol Aeroplane Company Ltd. where he had figured in the development of the *Olympus* and *Phoebus* jet engines as well as various prop-turbines. Prior to that phase he had spent ten years with the British Air Ministry, where his work had involved him in the early development of jet engine test procedures. He had not been long in Canada before his ability prompted his promotion, first to Chief Engineer, G/T (Gas Turbines), and subsequently to Vice-President Engineering and Chief Engineer at Orenda Engines Ltd. Upon his arrival in Canada, he was quickly involved in the many problems spawned by P.S. 13.

The development of a new jet engine is an extremely costly enterprise, a high risk venture made doubly uncertain by the tightly limited market available and by the vagaries of defence policy. Nowadays it would be virtually unheard of for a company to tackle such a project without government underwriting. In 1952 no such underwriting was available from the Canadian government, at least not until a company had demonstrated the practicability of its proposal by building a prototype that could display the performance predicted. When P.S. 13 began, it was strictly a private venture, financed by private capital. Obviously the Hawker-Siddeley Group could not rush into such a venture until the proposed design had been given close and sceptical scrutiny.

Winning the authorization of the Hawker-Siddeley Group's Design Council took Orenda's designers two full days of debate, starting October 14th, 1953. Orenda's engineers were proposing to break much new ground. In their bold design they had dispensed with the normal centre structure for a two-spool lightweight concept; the two rotors and shafts would have no centre bearings. Furthermore, except for their shafts the two compressors were to be constructed entirely of titanium, effecting a great weight saving.

The members of the Design Council focused most of their criticism on the two bearing shaft arrangement and the absence of the centre structure. However they allowed their criticism to be overborne by the manifest advantages of weight reduction, low cost and reliability. Early in December, 1953, authority was given to commit $300,000 for the purchase of three ingots of titanium (such ingots having lengthy delivery times). On January 13th, 1954, Orenda was given the authorization it needed: proceed with the detailed design and manufacture of three engines. Thus P.S. 13 was finally launched, as a private venture, with an initial limit of $3,500,000.

Orenda's earlier design, rejected by the RCAF, had aimed at producing an engine capable of 12,000 pounds thrust. P.S. 13 had the rather breathtaking objective of developing an engine with an air mass flow of 300 pounds per second, producing 20,000 pounds of dry thrust — 25,000 pounds with afterburner augmentation[1].

By utilizing various shortcuts it was hoped to have an engine on test in 12 months. This called for some highly efficient organization, and for such expedients as farming out the production of a supply of afterburners. Also, since the engine control system requirements were new and would require further time for adequate contract negotiations, the company decided to manufacture only "slave" controls for the first tests. Once it could demonstrate the basic engine, the company hoped to procure a government contract; but there were a great many hurdles to overcome before that aspiration could be realized.

Predictably, having set themselves such lofty targets, Orenda's engineers were not long in encountering problems, many of them stemming from the exploratory nature of much of the work. The problem of hydrogen embrittlement — another manifestation of

---

1. For much of the factual and technical information embodied in this Chapter I am indebted to Mr. Grinyer himself. He has written a series of lengthy, carefully worded letters answering my many questions. His writing is marked by understatement and precision. My appraisal of his own performance is based on other sources, and on the facts.

which we shall shortly be examining — presented itself at an early stage. The three titanium ingots originally purchased were found to have a hydrogen content of over one hundred parts in a million. A method of reducing this to a maximum of twenty parts in a million had to be devised. Lab experimentation showed that it could be done using a vacuum furnace at moderate temperature. Although the only one readily available to Orenda Engines Ltd. was of a very limited capacity (35 pounds), it provided the means by which the job was eventually done.

A memorable milestone was achieved in December, 1954. On December 5th the first P.S. 13 was delivered to test; and at 4:24 p.m. on the 19th of December, after the requisite preliminary checks had been made, flared into life and ran on its own power.

Charles Grinyer describes the discouraging developments that first took place:

"At about 6,000 r.p.m. a bad vibration band set in which it was impossible to run through. Both rotors were affected and so the remainder of the test was given to starting and running below the troubled band. This was a bad blow to our morale, as the results were quite contrary to our rig test results. In the end we chose to believe the rig tests and to look for some other explanation. Therefore, a very careful examination during the strip of the engine disclosed that oil had gained access to the high pressure compressor drum. This had occurred during the oil checks to the bearings. It left us with the puzzle as to why both rotors vibrated, and we were not to find the answer to this until some time later. Testing then followed a more or less routine pattern. This disclosed further troubles associated with titanium. First, the compressor blades began to seize in the slots of the titanium discs, and this was eventually overcome by silver plating the blade roots. The second fault was much more serious in that the titanium would catch fire from frictional rubs.

"It had been hoped and expected that the Canadian Government would place a contract after the demonstration run; and although this had been marred by the vibration trouble, it had been explained very quickly, and subsequent engine runs showed the oil had been the cause. Still, it was not before about mid-June, 1955, that such a contract was placed — by which time the cost of the project to the Company had risen to $8,500,000."

Under the terms of the contract the company was awarded approximately one-third of the costs incurred to that date. A further third was to be paid when the engine passed certain special milestone tests. This left Orenda with about one-third of its money in the project, for which it retained the right to sell the manufacturing rights on the engine outside Canada. It was shortly after the signing of the agreement that the name *Iroquois* was selected for the engine.

Starting in June, 1956, preliminary flight rating tests (P.F. R.T.'s) were run on the *Iroquois*, firstly with a Lucas fuel system and later with a Bendix. In each case the engine successfully passed a 50 hour P.F.R.T. at a rating of 16,000 pounds dry thrust, in other words, 80% of full designed power. Shortly after the Bendix test in September, 1956, Orenda lost one of the engines in a fire caused by the ignition of the titanium in the high pressure compressor. The first fire — there were several fires, and more than one engine lost before the engine was perfected — was the result of a blade failure, the piece becoming trapped and then "wiped" by the remaining blades. As Mr. Grinyer explains: "Because titanium is such a poor bearing material and a poor conductor of heat, this caused the material to heat up to the point of incandescence, and the air pressure blew a hole in the compressor casing. Then a torch effect occurred setting the whole engine on fire. Water failed to control the blaze, and we had to develop a powder method of fire control".

Having discovered by costly experience that titanium had its limitations for use in aero-engines, Grinyer's team decided to remove titanium from the stator rings and to substitute steel for titanium in the high compressor casing. This switch to steel carried a weight penalty of about 300 pounds, but over-all weight savings had been so substantial that this minor backsliding did not cause inordinate agonizing. A further modification was required to deal with the vibration problem. Tests had disclosed that if one shaft vibrated, the vibration was transferred to the other. By rig test the engineers discovered that this phenomenon could be avoided if the bearings were mounted in the same plane. With the bearing of the inner shaft directly below the bearing of the outer shaft any coupling effect between the shafts was avoided. Once the necessary modifications had been conceived and installed, testing proceeded with great success. In April, 1957, a test was run at 18,000 pounds dry thrust, and before the end of the year a 20,000 pound dry thrust test had been run. Orenda Engines Ltd. had proved its point, the *Iroquois* having achieved the tremendous full dry thrust performance called for by its ambitious designers. Of course much additional work remained to be done, much air testing, refinement and polishing.

The company had made arrangements, through the RCAF, for the loan of a B-47 from the United States Air Force for the flight testing of the *Iroquois*. In preparation for the flight testing, which was to be carried out by Canadian personnel, a crew headed by Mike Cooperslipper took conversion training on a B-47 at a Strategic Air Command base in the United States. The American Air Force was keenly interested in the potential of the *Iroquois* engine, hence in the early stages of P.S. 13 a close liaison had developed between the USAF and the Orenda team. The Assistant Secretary of the Air Force and various members of his staff frequently met with the Orenda group; and it was as a direct result of the excellent rapport developed that extensive wind tunnel test facilities and the B-47 aircraft had been made available to Orenda, free of charge.

In Canada the B-47 was modified by Canadair to carry the *Iroquois* engine. The great new power plant was to be carried in a special pod under the right tailplane of the aircraft — a distinct departure from the normal nose or under-the-fuselage installations frequently employed for flying test-beds. When the aircraft was rolled out of Canadair's workshops at Cartierville, Quebec, its newly trained crew were quickly given some graphic demonstrations of the tremendous potential of the *Iroquois*.

In the following weeks over 125 hours of air flight testing was carried out, supplementing the thousands of hours of ground running, and the *Iroquois* tested to the full altitude limits of the six-jet-engined B-47. Perhaps the simplest way to drive home the achievement of the Orenda designers is to point out that the single *Iroquois* engine mounted on the B-47 could deliver more than the total thrust of four of the B-47's jets[1]. The B-47 was not a supersonic aircraft, and was limited both in its forward speed and its altitude. An *Iroquois* with a limited rating of only 16,000 pounds dry thrust was more than sufficient for the B-47; and in fact, once airborne with the *Iroquois* started, it was necessary for the crew to throttle the normal J-47 engines right back to idling when the *Iroquois* was developing 16,000 pounds dry thrust.

Meanwhile, afterburner tests had been carried out, with rigs, both at Marquart in California, and at Malton. Once complete engine and afterburner controls had been secured from subcontractors, the full rating tests were carried out with engine and afterburner, about mid-1958. The Official Type Test, the passing of which would in effect constitute the RCAF's final acceptance of the power plant, was scheduled for February, 1959. Although there were no problems of any great magnitude manifesting themselves by the fall of 1958, Charles Grinyer suggested in September that the Type Test be deferred until August, 1959, to ensure that there would be no slip-up. He specified that certain work had to be completed to ensure the success of the Type Test. When he said that he would be ready to run the Type Test by August, 1959, he was fully satisfied that there would be no problem. In previous years he had sent ten different engines to Type Test, and without fail, all had received approval.

To understand what designers have to face, however, it should be pointed out that the Type Test was a lengthy and expensive process. Since it was the official way of approving an engine, it was controlled by the RCAF for all military applications. The term itself had come from the early British aero-engine days, and was carried over into the jet-engine era. The Type Test contemplated the following:

---

1. The 650 m.p.h. *Boeing* B-47 carried six General Electric J-47-GE-25 engines, each capable of 5970 lbs. (max.) thrust, and turning out 4478 lbs. each at the 75% cruise setting. The afterburner thrust of a fully rated *Iroquois* (25,000 lbs.) actually exceeded the cumulative maximum thrust of four J-47's by more than 1100 lbs.

A particular engine would have to be built for the test. All parts would be checked against production drawings, checked both as to dimensions and part numbers. As Charles Grinyer explains it:

"The test itself commences with a performance curve, and a given number of accelerations. The endurance part consists of 15 Ten-Hour periods, some of which cannot be run without a ten-hour interval, whilst others must have less than two hours between them. Total accelerations must exceed 100. No stop is permitted in the period, without the penalty of re-running that period. The thrust levels vary in the periods, and very complete records are taken.

"The test is completed by another performance curve. It is not usual to expect approval if the performance has decreased by more than 3%. Only limited service is permitted, and this has to be specified before the test starts. The engine is stripped down and parts examined for wear or failure. Dimensional checks are again made, and the parts again checked to the drawings. The Test is thought to represent about 400 hours of military flying."

With Mr. Grinyer's 100% batting average, his vast experience, and his habit of cautious understatement, it is not surprising that no one ever suggested that the *Iroquois* would not have passed its Type Test with flying colours.

For the sake of continuity and coherence we have followed the account of the development of the *Iroquois* engine to its final stages — at which point that development had entailed the expenditure of $87,000,000 and untold hours of effort and testing. The development of the *Arrow* airframe itself was equally arduous, equally replete with problems, and equally studded with technological triumphs of varying degree. But we must return to the point where only the general parameters of design had been determined.

Chapter 4

The general configuration of the *Arrow* having been determined
by the design specialists and confirmed through intensive wind tunnel
tests, it became the task of the production engineers and draftsmen
to translate the designers' bold conception into an actual airframe
that would perform within the extremely demanding parameters
designated as objectives. Item: A wing so thin that it seemed struc-
turally impossible with existing materials. Item: An airframe that
would function efficiently in an outside ground level temperature
range running from —65° F to +165° F. Item: An aircraft upon
which all routine maintenance operations could be performed quickly
and easily, the objective being the ability to change an engine in
less than thirty minutes — without hand tools or lifting tackle.

So demanding were the general dimensional and structural
limits that the CF-105 *Arrow* seemed at the outset an incongruent
assemblage of acute problems — problems moreover that would
yield only to incompatible solutions. Again, a description of all the
challenges to be surmounted would require a separate book. A few
representative examples will serve to suggest the host of others that
accompanied them.

Due to the magnitude of the forces involved in supersonic flying, it was essential that all flying controls be power driven. But hydraulic jacks of the conventional design were too thick to fit into the thin wing. Existing jacks of small enough diameter did not provide sufficient force with the accepted standard hydraulic pressures. Going to higher pressures would entail a long series of prohibitively expensive changes. The solution ultimately hit upon seemed to be to design exceptionally long, thin jacks with two or more compartments having pistons in tandem. But on the test bench the jacks bulged between the compartments, the outside boundaries being rigidly held by the diaphragms separating the compartments. To borrow one of E. J. Silling's apt descriptions: "It was like tying string around a sausage." The cure was to fashion stronger materials and change cylinder wall thickness. But even this required a difficult balancing of objectives, since thicker walls meant either increased external diameter — which would infringe upon precious space — or decreased internal diameter which would reduce piston area and lead to insufficient power. Only after lengthy experimentation was the right balance struck.

Linkages for the controls also proved difficult to design. The exceptionally thin wing imported a lack of space which prevented the structural engineers from making cross-sectional areas big enough to provide the necessary strength. Once again custom-built improved materials provided the answer. The engineers took the tensile strength of steel alloys and heat treatments to the ultimate limits available at that time, complementing the research and experimentation being done in the use of titanium. The latter metal was utilized not only for jet-engine blades — where A. V. Roe's process was so advanced that it eventually sold some $2,000,000 worth to U.S. engine manufacturers — but for certain critical areas of the airframe as well.

The extremely thin wing virtually precluded the sacrifice of further space for tanks, at least of the conventional type; so the interior of each wing was itself converted into a series of six integral fuel enclosures. Two rubber cell-type tanks in the fuselage completed the fuel stowage on the Mark 1, although on the projected Mark 2 provision was made for one external drop tank of 500 Imperial gallons, and the projected Mark 2A and Mark 3 were to be fitted with an additional internal tank to increase the range. The integral tank arrangement meant that within the "wet wing" all the electrical and hydraulic components were immersed in fuel, and this imported a host of sealing problems that had to be overcome. The flexing of the wing in flight posed further difficulties, causing leaks; but here the answer — when they discovered it — was to purchase from an American firm the rights to a process of injecting sealant along channels in the wing joints.

The drag parachute attachment which the *Arrow*, a "hot" aircraft, required during landings, was found to put unexpectedly heavy loads on the structure. These had to be provided for by modification. The related problem of designing a release mechanism of limited size for the chute took a considerable time to resolve. To prevent galling it was essential to have an extraordinarily hard metal surface on this device. The trigger mechanism and release control designs both posed novel problems as well. All the many challenges were met, often with highly ingenious responses, with the result that Avro ultimately took out a substantial number of patents on the new processes and designs involved.

The stipulation regarding easy engine maintenance spawned its own difficulties. These new engineering obstacles were addressed, and mastered, by having each engine clamped to rails. After removing the engine cowling, a trolley could be run up against the engine nacelle. The trolley had matching rails; thus, after releasing the self-sealing fuel lines and engine controls, by hand, the engine could be released and run out onto the trolley.

The supersonic configuration imported its own complex problem: flying stability had to be sacrificed. This meant that continual attitude corrections had to be made during flight. The essential automatic flight corrections were initiated through a long nose boom carrying the pitot and static tubes well out of the way of shock waves. This long boom was also fitted with small sensor vanes to control pitch, roll and yaw. The sensors operated magnetic switches that sent signals to a "black box" stability augmentation system built by Minneapolis Honeywell, which in turn operated the hydraulic valves on the control jacks whenever the aircraft attitude changed slightly in flight. Thus the necessary corrections were made even during maneuvers. Nevertheless, even when the theoretical answers had been produced, the engineers encountered new problems stemming from the almost continuous flexing and vibrating of the boom. Again much experimentation with titanium provided the answer. The Minneapolis Honeywell "black box" was to function flawlessly in time; but early in the flight test program it was to provide one stunning surprise. Meanwhile there were other engineering barriers to circumvent.

At the supersonic speeds contemplated for the *Arrow*, it was essential that a minutely gauged response be obtained from the flight controls. To provide the most accurate response, signals to the hydraulic control valves were provided by strain gauges which measured the minute movements of the control column under the pressure applied by the pilot. The power-operated flying controls were activated by valves operated from the pilot's controls; therefore the pilot had no "feel" available for judging the very substantial loads imposed on the airframe. Artificial "feel" was fed into the pilot's controls by a device containing springs, dampers, and weights, which read G-loads during maneuvers. A complete emergency control system operating the control valves had also to be fashioned.

Another challenging feature was a device whose objective was to keep control surface movement proportional to flying speed. For example, full operation of the rudder pedal might move the rudder through an arc of 15° at taxying speeds or while landing. At supersonic speeds, the same pedal movement would move the control surface only 1°, giving the same in-flight response. This was done by measuring airspeed with an electronic device which in turn operated a motor that varied the control linkage.

Fashioning the undercarriage for the new aircraft raised yet other questions of technique, and carried the crews to new levels of expense in that field. To the layman an aircraft's landing gear is a mundane item. This is definitely not so to the pilot, dependent upon its proper functioning for a safe return to earth. And to the engineer required to design and manufacture the necessary undercarriage, it can present — as it did with the *Arrow* — a whole range of specialized problems. In the *Arrow's* case these flowed from weight limitation, from extra stress associated with higher landing speeds, and from the fact that the thin wing afforded almost no stowage and the fuselage only a limited amount.

Harry Ralph, presently a consulting engineer in Kirkland, Washington, joined A. V. Roe in September, 1953, then moved to Dowty Equipment of Canada at Ajax, Ontario, a year later when that company was awarded the contract for the *Arrow* landing gear. In response to a query about the problems encountered in producing the gear, he pointed out that development of the ultra high tensile alloy steel which was found necessary for the relatively slender gear was an extremely expensive proposition. The ultimate strength of material ranged from 260,000 to 280,000 pounds per square inch.

As was the case with so many other features of the aircraft, many new manufacturing techniques were found necessary to make this material a practical proposition when utilized for an aircraft landing gear. After the application of the sophisticated heat treatment given the alloy, it was found that a thin, hard and brittle layer (the "hydrogen embrittlement") tended to form all over the work piece. This layer had to be removed, since it created poor fatigue qualities in the part concerned. As a result, every item designed and produced from this alloy had to be machined approximately 95% all over prior to heat treatment, and then machined 100% all over again in order to get rid of the hydrogen embrittlement layer. One needs no technical background to appreciate the extra difficulty — and the radically increased cost — of producing each part twice, in effect, with only the final machining bringing the component down to the specified tolerance, after application of a preliminary machining and a sophisticated heat treatment.

Work on other parts of the aircraft ran into comparable obstacles. The tremendous ground level outside heat range ($-65°F$ to $+165°$ F) within which the aircraft had to function efficiently produced bizarre effects on ball bearings, for example. E. J. Silling has provided a full description: Ball bearings pressed into cranks at ambient temperatures simply fell out at $+165°$ F. If the bearings were pressed in at the high temperature limit, they jammed solidly at $-65°$ F. The engineers found, after considerable experimentation, that if the bearings were made to extremely close limits they could be made to work. But then no bearing manufacturer would even attempt to produce bearings to the tolerances demanded. Eventually the company persuaded one manufacturer to provide suitable bearings by way of "selective assembly". This too was extremely costly, but it worked. By selecting balls which were dead on the minus tolerance size, then installing them only in ball races which had come out exactly on the plus tolerance limit, the assemblies could be made to function efficiently over the whole temperature range. One more problem was laid to rest.

Similar difficulties were faced with control cables. When the airframe was cold, the slack control wires hung in festoons. When a test airframe approached the upper temperature limit, the heat pulled the wires so tight that pulley brackets collapsed and fittings were torn loose. The basic reason for the phenomenon was the different coefficients of expansion for aluminum and steel, the expansion of steel being much less, for a given change in temperature, than that of aluminum. The solution for this problem was found to be self-adjusting cable quadrants. Although these were already in existence, many of them had to be substantially modified to fit in tight places.

Perhaps even this microscopic sampling of the multitudinous problems encountered will serve to suggest the heavy technological demands made upon the design and fabricating teams. It may serve as well to hint at the ingenuity, industry, and general talent of the highly skilled work force that had been mustered to implement the RCAF's vision of its new aerial weapon.

Chapter 5

In 1953 Air Marshal Curtis, now 60 years of age, retired from the RCAF, and promptly began a new career as Vice-President of A. V. Roe Canada Ltd. (In later years he was persuaded to embark upon still another career as Chancellor of Toronto's York University from 1960-1968.) As Vice-Chairman of the Board of A. V. Roe one of his concerns in 1953 and 1954 was to oversee (although he had no direct responsibility for it) the whole *Arrow* project, the program to which much of his energy had ultimately been directed as the RCAF's Chief of Air Staff.

While work was progressing during 1954 it was learned that the Russians had developed a jet bomber, and that they had exploded a nuclear bomb. This latter accomplishment the Russians thus demonstrated several years earlier than had been anticipated in the west, thanks to some diligent spying and the assistance of traitors. The threat against which the *Arrow* had been pointed seemed to be developing exactly as anticipated, except for the speed of the Russians' progress, which lent a further spur to the strenuous efforts being made at Avro.

While the *Arrow* had been progressing to the point where production drawings were being channeled along to the manufacturing section, the government had been moving to shore up the aircraft's financial prospects, already so worrisome to C. D. Howe. The Honourable Ralph Campney, Minister of Defence in the administration of Prime Minister Louis St. Laurent, journeyed to Washington to speak to his counterpart there and ascertain whether the Americans would be interested in purchasing the *Arrow*, assuming the finished machine met its highly impressive projected specifications. The American government officials gave warm encouragement to the production of this seemingly remarkable machine — but no firm commitment to buy. Nevertheless, the Canadian government took considerable comfort from this moral support.

Mention has already been made of the setbacks that occurred in 1955 with the USAF abandoning development of the Curtiss-Wright J-67 engine, after the abandonment by Rolls Royce of the engine that had been first choice for the Mark I *Arrow*. Ultimately the Pratt & Whitney J-75 was selected, and A. V. Roe's management could turn its attention to other problem areas.

The RCAF's insistence on switching from the Hughes MX-1179 weapons system to the new ASTRA had carried the day with the government despite the company's strong recommendation to the contrary. The *Sparrow II* missiles that were to complement the new system were in the early development stage in Douglas Aircraft plants in the U.S. They were to be adapted in Canada to their role with the ASTRA-equipped *Arrow* by Canadair Limited and Douglas Aircraft, working from the basic U.S. design. Primarily the Canadian companies were to concentrate their efforts on the guidance and fire and flight control systems — at least that was the original intention.

The RCAF's seeming desire to go first class in every respect was readily understandable — in fact, on purely military grounds it was undoubtedly the proper decision. They were working on what promised to be the most advanced interceptor in the western world — why take the Hughes system with *Falcon* missiles when the ASTRA with *Sparrow IIs* promised more efficiency and hence maximum utilization of the superlative weapons platform represented by the *Arrow?* The government's acquiescence was harder to understand, on purely practical grounds, because the development of the ASTRA and the *Sparrow II* held high potential for complex problems and soaring cost. And here, according to Carl V. Lindow, the government's officers did an uncharacteristically inefficient job in their negotiating and writing of specifications. Lindow, who was one of Avro's senior engineers[1] (now retained as a consultant by Boeing) is critical in describing this phase:

"It was Armament Engineering, also specifying the ASTRA electronic system, that was to cause the cost of the weapons system to escalate and put it in jeopardy even if the government had not changed. These features, the *Sparrow II* missile with its guidance and the ASTRA advanced electronics had a very significant contribution to the cost of the system. There were other missiles and other electronic systems that could be procured more or less off the shelf which would have been highly satisfactory and about 95% as effective.

"In particular, the ASTRA system contract won by RCA was ill-conceived in that the initial contract statement of work definition asked for only about 10% of the work that was ultimately required to develop the system. The system specified would have been by far the highest performing system in the world with a one megawatt peak power magnetron — capable of automatically flying the airplane onto its target, [with] ground mapping capability, data link and every other facility imaginable. RCA performed technically in an excellent manner, but perhaps could have furnished more information on what the ultimate cost was going to be. When it was realized that the ultimate cost of developing the ASTRA Fire Control System was going to be between 100 and 200 million dollars the program was cancelled and the Hughes . . . radar fire control system adopted along with the Hughes *(Falcon)* missiles which was what we at Avro had advocated at the outset. These decisions resulted in a very small degradation of the weapons system

1. The main design team of Avro's earlier and highly successful CF-100 had been the team of Project Engineer John Frost, Bob Lindley, Jim Chamberlin and Carl V. Lindow.

capability — with a very large saving of cost."

These were the views of one highly competent engineer[1]; but the full picture requires a glimpse of the responsibilities and efforts of those directly answerable for the aircraft's weapons system. Air Vice-Marshal John Easton held several senior appointments in the RCAF during the period 1945-1960, some of them involving direct responsibility in this field. In 1951 he was brought back to the Headquarters Staff with the appointment of Chief of Armament. In August, 1958, having left the Chief of Armament's post for some time to act as Chief of Operational Requirements and later as Chief of Telecommunications, he came back into the program as the Air Member for Technical Services.

In the earlier stages of this period, he points out, the RCAF was in control of the various research and development programs, and the Department of Defence Production was its contractual agent. Before the end of the period the Defence Research Board had been formed, and there was reorganization within the RCAF itself. As a result, the RCAF became further removed from the contractor, with the consequence that it lost the quick response time that is so important in the development phase of any program.

One of the first points that had to be considered by those responsible for the new aircraft's weapons system was the sharply reduced reaction time that advances in aviation had imported. Thus, the armament staff had carried out careful studies of the needs of an aircraft weapons system that would work in the early warning and ground control defence system. As A.V.M. Easton points out: "With aircraft closing speeds approaching Mach 4 plus, and both aircraft supersonic, . . . the time left to detect, get to the attack position, and deliver the attack without losing any opportunity, becomes very small. If you limit yourself to pursuit only, then penetration of the defence area becomes excessive and allows the attacker to optimize his defence against you — such as countermeasures ECM, retro-firing weapons, etc. Consequently, if nuclear weapons are being delivered by the attacker, you would be considered less than prudent if you did not optimize your defence

---

1. Lindow was Engineering Program Manager on the aircraft's weapons system.

weapons system. In addition to what has been said, the best chance of destruction of the enemy's nuclear weapon is the use of nuclear warheads in your airborne defensive weapons . . ."

Reviewing the state of the art at that time, A.V.M. Easton went on to mention that "Sperry, Collins had automatic flight and landing systems in use, as did some others, such as PYE of the U.K. and RCA in the United States. Also, inertial navigation systems were reaching a high state of development, with some systems in use. Map reading capability in radars had been in use for some time, e.g., bombing radars. In fact, the CF-104 had all these features. The *Sparrow* missiles were in U.S. Navy use and the *Sparrow II* was in an advanced stage of development; it had the range and control and warhead capabilities that were necessary, and fire control was no problem — having been in use for some years. The MX-1179 and *Falcon* missiles were good, but short in three areas. The power of the radar was insufficient in our estimation to meet the range and countermeasure requirements, and the missile [fell short] in range, countermeasure and payload for the period 1958 onward, against the type of threat to be expected."

"We put all our requirements together and approached the Hughes Aircraft Co., who had done such a good job for us on the MG2 system in the CF-100, to see if they would be interested in taking on development of the system. The outcome of the meetings spread over three days in Culver City, California, was that it was MX-1179 and *Falcon* or they were really not interested. However, other companies were approached, such as RCA, Westinghouse, Minneapolis Honeywell, Sperry, G. E. Ltd., and Emmerson. These companies had been building radars and fire control systems for both USAF and USN. These companies were interested, and put forward proposals to integrate the fire control and flight control systems. The higher powered magnetron was generally accepted as necessary to get the added range and greater security in the face of ECM (electronic countermeasures). As a result of the various proposals, the ASTRA program was called up."

Reviewing the comments of Carl Lindow and A.V.M. Easton, each an expert in his field, it is easy to understand and reconcile the small degree of divergence in their views. Carl Lindow was presumably interested primarily in getting the best possible flying machine airborne, and critical of factors jeopardizing that objective. Air Vice-Marshal John Easton regarded it as a waste not to utilize the potential of the aircraft (weapons platform) to the full, particularly in view of the performance and weapons capabilities to be anticipated from the bomber threat. In retrospect, he parts company with Carl Lindow over the latter's belief that the difference in performance between the two weapons systems and their missiles can accurately be quantified and expressed in simple terms. He underlined the point that the *Falcon* missile was more vulnerable to countermeasures, and concluded:

"If the ASTRA system had been carried to completion it would have been superior to the MX-1179 in range of radar, ability to withstand electronic countermeasures, adaptability to other weapons such as *Sparrow II*, the British missiles, and some others with ranges which could exploit the all-round choice for opportunity of attack on the hostile aircraft. Consequently, trying to put any percentage figure on comparative effectiveness could be misleading. For example, I think that the chance of frontal attack with MX-1179 and *Falcon* in the environment I mentioned above would be zero."

If A.V.M. Easton, and other RCAF officers consulted regarding the various phases of the development of the *Arrow* and its weapons system, differ with Mr. Lindow on the importance of ASTRA in the ultimate denouement, they are definitely at one with him in their refusal to pretend that they were infallible, or that even with the benefit of hindsight they cannot see where their decisions could profitably have been modified. Both sides are in agreement on the point that there were cogent reasons for the decisions they elected to make, and that, at the time, they believed those decisions to be the best ones, all things considered.

That the new missile program, i.e., involvement in the development of the *Sparrow II*, commended itself to the government was rather surprising, since the government was in the process of persuading itself to cancel the *Velvet Glove* Canadian missile program that it had backed for years, and must have been fully aware of the potential costs if the parameters of the program were not rigidly controlled.

Douglas Aircraft Co., which had designed the airframe for *Sparrow I*, was to perform the same function for *Sparrow II*. Sperry Gyroscope Co. had been the prime contractor on the *Sparrow I* development, working in concert with Douglas and Aerojet. Over a period of approximately ten years, bringing that project to the operational level had consumed the sobering total of 4,000,000 engineering man hours. Now Douglas was embarking upon the development of *Sparrow II* so that it could be used for the projected naval interceptor Douglas was under contract to build, the F-5D *Sky Lancer*. Apart from Canadair and Douglas, the companies in Canada who were to work on adapting the *Sparrow II* for use with the Avro CF-105 *Arrow* included Avro Aircraft Ltd., Canadian Westinghouse Company Ltd., Computing Devices of Canada Ltd. and DeHavilland Aircraft of Canada.

This decision by the government to proceed with *Sparrow II* missile development — unless it was very sharply circumscribed — represented yet another incipient reversal in policy. In 1956 the Liberal government proceeded to terminate a most extensive program, begun in 1951. Project *Velvet Glove* had been designed to develop and bring into production in Canada a missile system upon which considerable initial research had been done by its own agency, the Canadian Armament Research and Development Establishment. A great deal of expertise had been accumulated by the Canadian firms involved, and a substantial measure of success achieved; but just before the weapon was to go into production the government of Prime Minister St. Laurent cancelled the project, flushing five years of effort and $24,000,000 of the taxpayers' money down the drain.

Aimed in a different direction, the Canadian missile industry was sent off again, this time engaged in the adaptation and development of *Sparrow II*. Unfortunately, some months later the United States government abandoned the *Sparrow II*, leaving the full burden of its extremely expensive development on the companies adapting it for use with ASTRA and the CF-105 *Arrow* — in effect the Canadian government.

Despite the diligence of A. V. Roe's management, headed by its President and General Manager, Crawford Gordon, and notwithstanding the innovative industry of its highly skilled work force, the *Arrow* program, through suffering unavoidable setbacks and government directed modifications, had encountered the sharply rising costs invariably associated with those business hazards. From the outset the program had been subject to frequent government review. Under the St. Laurent Cabinet it was renewed at each stage on the clear understanding that it could be terminated on very short notice at any time. Nevertheless, the highly encouraging technological progress induced the government to continue its approvals in spite of the fact that in 1955 the funds then available, $211,000,000, had promised to be insufficient to complete the development originally estimated by C. D. Howe and Avro's management at $100,000,000. Additional engineering costs were a large factor in this escalated estimate, of course, coupled with rising labour charges and higher material and processing costs.

In a speech in the House of Commons the Honourable George Pearkes later emphasized that at this time the company had been informed by the Liberal government that ". . . while there were to be some 40 CF-105 airframes produced at a cost of $191,000,000, and 14 *Iroquois* engines at a cost of $70,000,000, it was to be understood that the program for both the airframes and the engines could be halted and abandoned at any appropriate stages if this was found to be expedient or necessary". The fact of the matter was that the St. Laurent government was checking the program carefully every six months because of the extremely heavy costs involved, costs unprecedented in Canadian peacetime Defence expenditures.

Pearkes went on to point out that by 1955 the St. Laurent government had calculated that approximately $300,000,000 would be required for development, with an additional $1,544,000,000 to be earmarked for the equipping of 15 squadrons — instead of the original 19 contemplated. The number of squadrons to be equipped had been reduced because the unit cost of the *Arrow* had gone up from the original estimated maximum of $2,000,000 to $2,600,000 per aircraft. As the already heavy cost burden increased, the Liberal government's reservations about the project became even more pronounced.

Its uneasiness was compounded by further information it began to receive late in 1955, to the effect that American aircraft plants, with United States government backing, had proceeded with the development of aircraft alleged to have somewhat similar performances to that of the *Arrow*. The F-100 *Super Sabre* and the F-102 *Delta Dagger* (after re-design known as the F106 *Delta Dart)* had passed the drawing board and prototype stages and were approaching production.

The F-100, the world's first supersonic fighter, had been underway well before the *Arrow*, and the first prototype had actually flown at Edwards Air Force Base on May 25th, 1953. Although supersonic, its speed was far below that intended for the *Arrow*. Convair's *Delta Dagger*, the F-102, had flown in prototype form five months after the F-100, in October, 1953; but it had succumbed initially to the supersonic flight instability with which the *Arrow's* engineers had grappled, and it ultimately had to be re-designed — and was further refined as the F-106 *Delta Dart*. Again, the USAF's specification simply required from these two aircraft a speed in excess of Mach 1, not the Mach 2 figure laid down for the first *Arrow*[1]. Although these aircraft differed significantly in several respects from the proposed *Arrow*, and were not designed to achieve several of the performance characteristics demanded by the RCAF in its specification, they made it clear that the *Arrow* would not have the field to itself and would be up against strong sales competition when it was ready for squadron service. This decreasing likelihood of easy sales to the United States, sales which would have enabled Avro to reduce significantly the heavy unit cost associated with the now contemplated run of 500 aircraft, deepened the St. Laurent cabinet's concern over the financial burden this aircraft would represent.

---

1. The revised F-106 first flew on December 26th, 1956. With the new Pratt & Whitney J-75-P-17 engine the F-106 eventually achieved a maximum speed of Mach 2.3.

As 1956 wound to a close and 1957 arrived, with its prospects of a federal election, Avro's progress against the complex problems imported by Mach 2 supersonic flight continued satisfactorily, even if not at the pace originally hoped for. Before the beginning of 1957 it was clear that 1955's target of a first flight in May, 1957, would not be met; and shortly it became equally apparent that the alternative date of August, 1957, would also prove too optimistic. But at least the end was in sight, and ground trials on a finished aircraft could finally be scheduled for October, 1957.

In the interval, however, certain changes in the political and military situation took place. They were critically important changes.

Chapter 6

The Canadian federal election of June 10th, 1957, produced election returns that surprised the majority of the electorate. To the somewhat complacent Liberal government of Louis St. Laurent the result was a shattering upset. John Diefenbaker's Conservative Party achieved a plurality, and on June 21st were sworn in as a minority government. The Conservatives had been out of office federally for over 20 years, and although John Diefenbaker himself, and several of his new Cabinet Ministers, had seen considerable service as opposition Members of Parliament, the feel of the reins of power was strange to their grasp. The federal civil service had been a Liberal fief seemingly from time immemorial, and the new relationships established between the political masters and their permanent Deputy Ministers were not universally those of full confidence and trust[1].

---

1. A similar situation obtained with respect to a few leaders of the Armed Forces. One of Prime Minister Diefenbaker's Cabinet Ministers described to me a scene he personally witnessed that fall when the reigning monarch, Elizabeth II, opened the Canadian Parliament for the first time. As the Prime Minister approached to pass a group of VIP's seated with their wives, a very senior RCAF officer turned to his wife and said "That's one son of a bitch I don't stand up for".

The new Minister of Defence, the Honourable George R. Pearkes, was a man of many parts. The Victoria Cross he was entitled to wear attested sufficiently to his personal courage. He coupled with that attribute an easy and modest charm, an abundant quota of fairness, and great diligence. He was quickly apprised of the essential inside information regarding the *Arrow* program, and of developments in Canada's NATO relationships and responsibilities. With little breathing space he found himself being briefed for his role in John Foster Dulles' impending visit to Canada. With that meeting behind him he had scarcely had time to digest all the financially significant minutiae of the *Arrow* program when the Russians launched the first intercontinental ballistic missile on August 27th, 1957.

Before the implications of that event had been long pondered the Russians followed it with a startling surprise by launching *Sputnik I* on October 4th, 1957, from the launching pad at their Baikonur space facility. The radio waves that emanated from that triumphant satellite were as nothing compared with the shock waves it sent through every foreign office and military establishment in the western democracies.

In the United States humiliation at being thrust into second place by technologically superior Russian space scientists was overshadowed by military concern at their startling accomplishment, for the polished aluminum of the world's first satellite, 23 inches in diameter, encompassed inner equipment that brought its total weight up to 184 pounds. America's first satellite, when it belatedly took to the air, was little more than one-ninth the weight of *Sputnik*. By applying their own calculations of launcher-to-satellite weight, American scientists estimated the weight of the Russian launching rocket at something over 100 tons, far superior in motive force to anything then within American capabilities.

The fact that *Sputnik* was much larger than anything the western democracies had considered practicable bespoke a much more advanced military threat should rocket engines of that size be applied to ICBMs. Shaken western military advisers began a thoroughgoing reappraisal and updating of the relative strengths of the geat powers. It seemed that Russia could fairly claim the title of First World Power, a title that had seemed firmly in America's grasp in the first years after Hiroshima and after the hydrogen bomb. Many journalists were over-hasty in according the palm unreservedly and immediately to the Russians, and over-all there was a general tendency amongst their number to over-react and move towards the ranks of the determinedly pessimistic. This climate of opinion could scarcely fail to have some effect in due course on American and Canadian politicians.

But at Malton on October 4th, 1957, the remarkable achievement of the Russians took a distant second place to an event of much more immediate importance. The roll-out ceremony of the first *Arrow* was to take place before a hangar whose doors had spawned many a *Lancaster* only a dozen years before. In those dozen years, partly under the impetus of Air Marshal Curtis' vision, the Canadian military aircraft industry had moved from the 200 m.p.h. *Lancaster* to the *Arrow*, an aircraft, so rumour had it, calculated to make the *Lancaster* look like something from the shop of the Wright Brothers.

At ten minutes past three that afternoon, a crowd of 1000 VIPs and almost 10,000 other highly interested spectators saw the Honourable George Pearkes, V.C., pull the symbolic golden cord, and a few seconds later the first CF-105 moved forward from the deep shadows in the hangar, broke through the bunting into the bright sunlight, and took up a position in the centre of the roped off enclosure. Here she was to bask briefly in the gaze of her admirers before embarking upon extensive ground trials. This aircraft, representing the first fruit of almost six years' challenging labour, invited close scrutiny.

She was clearly a winner. Pilots know that nine times out of ten when a new aeroplane truly looks like a winner it performs accordingly — provided it has not been short-changed in its power plant. Measured against that criterion *Arrow* 25201, the first of the initial series of 37 on Avro's production line, was assuredly a winner, for she was an impeccable white vision of aerodynamic loveliness. To a pilot's eye she exuded an almost mesmerizing air of grace, power, efficiency and pride.

The pilot's cockpit of the *Arrow* stood 14 feet six inches over

Right: *The fixed geometry inlet ramp of the Arrow is clearly shown here. The chisel-edged style of the 12 degree intake ramp is apparent, as are the perforations on its face, the latter comprising a form of boundary layer bleed.*
(AIR AND SPACE DIVISION, NATIONAL MUSEUM, OTTAWA)

Below: *Much supersonic flight research was done with free-flight radio controlled models. Here one is being prepared for launch on the nose of a rocket.*
(Via P. J. BRENNAN)

Above: *The great moment for the first public appearance of the Arrow approaches — October 4th, 1957, at Avro's Malton plant.* (CAF)

Below: *This photo of the Arrow, taken towards the end of the ceremony, affords a very good view of the Arrow's elegant profile.* (CAF)

Above: *The cord is cut and the first Arrow rolls forward into the sunlight to the delight of the admiring throng.*

(Via P. J. BRENNAN)

Below: *Arrow No. 1 poses for her admirers. Among the dignitaries on the platform at the left were the Minister of National Defence, George Pearkes, V.C., and the Chief of Air Staff, Air Marshal Hugh Campbell. Note the RCAF band seated in the foreground.* (AIR AND SPACE DIVISION, NATIONAL MUSEUM, OTTAWA)

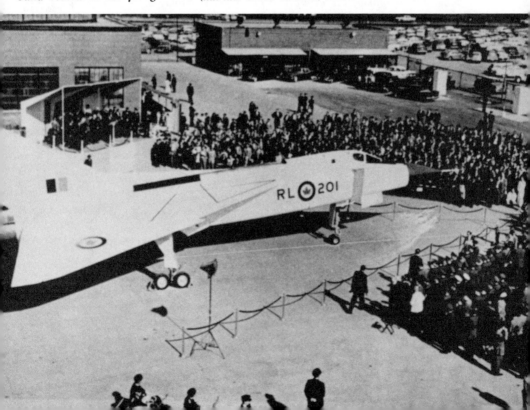

Above: *The clean lines of the Arrow would impress even the layman. To the enthusiast she was an impeccable white vision of aerodynamic loveliness.* (CAF)

Below: *With the speeches over the crowd presses forward for an even closer look. The height of the aircraft is graphically displayed — to a pilot's eye the Arrow exuded an almost mesmerizing air of grace, power, efficiency and pride.* (CAF)

Above: *The plan view obtained by the photographers on the hangar roof is shown here. The leading edge notch and leading edge extension of the Arrow's Delta wing are clearly evident. These features were designed to control the spanwise flow of the boundary layer air.* (CAF)

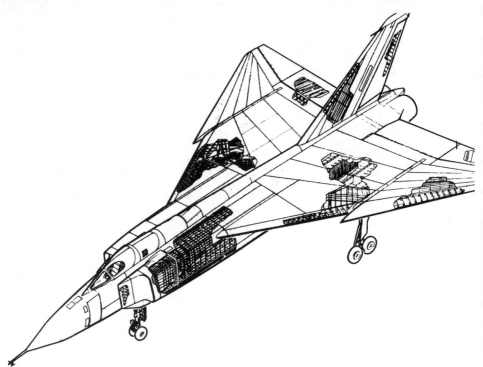

Above: *This cut-away drawing gives some impression of the basic structural design of the aircraft.*

(Via P. J. BRENNAN)

Below: *With the roll-out ceremony complete, Arrow No. 1 leaves to begin the ground test program. The outline of the large weapons bay, which could be completely replaced in minutes, is clearly visible. The wheel wells in the thin wing also show to advantage.*

(CAF)

Above: *This view shows the afterburner and tailcone section. Worth noting are the blunt trailing edges of the control surfaces, so designed to improve their effectiveness at high Mach numbers.* (CAF)

Below: *Ground handling trials being carried on in November 1957. Note that the original weapons pack has been replaced and repainted, and that the intake lip has been painted black. The unorthodox clam-shell type cockpit canopy is well displayed.* (AIR AND SPACE DIVISION, NATIONAL MUSEUM, OTTAWA)

Above: *The Arrow taxies past with the rectangular panels of its speed brakes extended.* (AIR AND SPACE DIVISION, NATIONAL MUSEUM, OTTAWA)

Below: *The first low speed taxi trials took place in late December, 1957. Note the large deflection of the control surfaces — evidently under test.* (AIR AND SPACE DIVISION, NATIONAL MUSEUM, OTTAWA)

the runway; (the CF-100's comparable measurement was ten feet seven inches); the fin stretched up another seven feet to 21 feet three inches. Excluding the long nose boom, she was 77 feet 9.65 inches long from the nose to the trailing edge of the fin, some 25 feet longer than the CF-100. She was tailless, i.e., without a horizontal stabilizer, which enhanced the clean appearance of the empennage. From wingtip to wingtip she measured 50 feet at the widest point, and her main undercarriage had a track with a width of 25 feet 5.66 inches. The run between the nose wheel and the main landing gear was 30 feet one inch.

Viewed from the front, the modest anhedral of four degrees on the high delta wing (embodied in the design to reduce landing gear length) contributed to her overall impression of some speedy bird of prey, poised hawk-like for a thrust from steel tendoned legs into takeoff and pursuit. A group of favoured insiders who were perched across the top of the hangar got an equally impressive plan view, the clean angularity of the 1200 square foot white delta wing providing a striking suggestion of arrowhead speed. There was no doubt about it, the CF-105's sophisticated dash marked it as a champion. The roll-out ceremony, belated though it was, was quickly transformed into the harbinger of success.

George Pearkes sensed the feeling, and expressed the general sentiment in his brief remarks. He gave recognition to the gleaming 30-ton *Arrow* as a milestone in the annals of Canadian aviation, and styled it enthusiastically "the symbol of a new era for Canada in the air".

The new Chief of Air Staff, Air Marshal Hugh Campbell, followed with a significant endorsement, saying, in part:

"The planned performance of this aircraft is such that it can effectively meet and deal with any likely bomber threat to this continent over the next decade . . . Because this aircraft . . . is a twin engine, two-place machine, and because it will embody what will be the most modern equipment in the airborne interception and fire control fields, it should have an inherent flexibility in operations and promising future development potential. For these reasons we look to it to fill a great need in the air defence system in the years to come."

The following day's newspaper photographs of the spectacular new fighter gave Canadians cause for pride. A few short weeks before, on July 27th, 1957, John Foster Dulles had made his first call upon the new Conservative administration of John Diefenbaker. After a five-day interval, Defence Minister George Pearkes had made the somewhat surprising announcement that Canada's government had agreed to the proposal earlier put forward by the United States that the two countries link their continental air defence establishments in a single combined North American Air Defence Command.

The surprise, it should be noted, stemmed only from the speed with which the decision had been made and announced. The preceding Liberal government had declined to take precipitate action on a proposal with such far-reaching implications, particularly with an election impending. But under the Diefenbaker administration, NORAD had been launched immediately, and became operational at its Colorado Springs headquarters only a few days after the *Arrow's* roll-out ceremony at Malton. Canada's then Chief of Air Staff, Air Marshal Roy Slemon, a talented airman who was highly regarded by colleagues on both sides of the border, had been appointed Deputy Commander of NORAD, and it was apparent that the appointment carried genuine responsibility. Seeing the photographs of their new supersonic interceptor gave Canadians a heightened sense of pride: the *Arrow* was an assurance that Canada, traditionally one of the most air-minded nations in the world, would do more than simply hold its end up in the NORAD compact. It would provide NORAD not only with a highly qualified Deputy Commander and the support of a strong RCAF, but also with an aircraft that gave promise of being the finest, most sophisticated interceptor in the world.

The Queen formally opened the first session of the twenty-third parliament of Canada on October 14th, 1957. The speech from the throne made a brief reference to national defence:

"My ministers believe that Canada's active participation in the North Atlantic Treaty Organization is essential for the preservation of peace. You will accordingly be asked to maintain modern defence forces in being which, together with those of our allies, will continue to act as a deterrent to attack upon any part of that alliance."

It then went on to presage an increased level of social services, a policy which was to exercise a distinct, if indirect, influence on the *Arrow:*

". . . Accordingly you will be asked to increase old age security pensions and to shorten the period of residence required to qualify for them. Changes will be proposed in the terms of assistance offered to provincial governments to enable them to increase the payments to be made under the Old Age Assistance Act, the Blind Persons Act and the Disabled Persons Act to a corresponding level.

"You will also be asked to increase the scale of war veterans allowances and to enlarge the groups to whom they are paid."

Other government measures were proposed to stabilize farm prices and to make provision for a system of cash advances for stored grain.

These progressive measures were undeniably overdue. They were also expensive, and they were to make their cumulative contribution in due course to the Diefenbaker government's financial problems. To cite the impact of one of them: when the Honourable J. W. Monteith subsequently introduced the legislation to amend the Old Age Security Act, increasing payments from $46 per month to $55, and reducing the qualifying residence requirement from 20 years to ten, he estimated it would cost an additional $95.5 million.

Meanwhile, at Malton the ground trials of the *Arrow* went on apace during November. By December the taxying tests were begun, the final, if somewhat lengthy prelude to the great moment everyone at Avro had strained for — the moment of truth when the *Arrow* would rise from the runway and test its wings on the first flight. As that moment drew nearer the instability of the political situation surrounding it became more pronounced, in marked contrast to the majority government stability that had obtained during the *Arrow's* first four and a half years.

In the House of Commons both Conservatives and Liberals knew there was every likelihood they would shortly be into another election campaign, in an attempt on the part of the Conservatives to wrest a clear-cut mandate from the electorate, and on the part of the Liberals to restore their former hegemony. The next round was not to be long delayed.

The Liberals went through the process of picking a new leader to replace Louis St. Laurent, who had resigned the party leadership. To succeed that avuncular and gracious gentleman, Lester Pearson was selected on January 16th, 1958. Prime Minister Diefenbaker shortly gave him a harsh and humiliating baptism of fire in the House, scoring savagely against an ill-advised motion that Pearson's cohorts had persuaded him to make. Following up his advantage the Prime Minister sought and obtained a dissolution of Parliament on February 1st, 1958, and a new election campaign was on. The election itself was scheduled for March 31st, and that day's balloting brought the Conservatives the greatest majority ever given any party in the Canadian House of Commons — 208 out of 265 seats.

Six days before Prime Minister Diefenbaker experienced this unprecedented political triumph the *Arrow's* designers and builders prepared to celebrate what was thus far their greatest achievement.

Chapter 7

On March 25th, 1958, the great day arrived for Avro and its chief test pilot. Jan Zurakowski finished his cockpit check at 9:30 a.m., and in an atmosphere of tense expectation taxied out for takeoff on Malton's newly lengthened (11,050 feet) Runway 32. Appropriately, Canada's most advanced aircraft was in the hands of one of the world's best test pilots.

Jan Zurakowski had already won his spurs as a first rank test pilot. He had demonstrated his right to membership in the select circle that included John Cunningham, Jeffrey Quill, Mutt Somers and Geoffrey de Havilland. During his World War II service in the RAF Zurakowski had shot down six enemy aircraft. When the fighting was over he had been hired as a test pilot by Gloster Aircraft, and had been chief test pilot on the Gloster *Meteor*. His skill, nerve, and lightning reflexes built him an impressive reputation. Hence when Avro went looking for a first class test pilot to display their new CF-100 to best advantage they sent to England and induced "Zura" to come to Malton as one of their senior test pilots[1]. Now he was being called upon to test fly an aircraft that promised, on paper, to be the most advanced in the western world.

1. Zurakowski in due course became Chief Experimental Test Pilot under Don Rogers who was Chief Test Pilot. When "Zura" was promoted he showed up with his new picture badge and title — under which he had solemnly added his own line: "NEW JOB . . . NO NEW PAY".

Just before 10:00 a.m. Zura was in position on Runway 32. Potocki and Woodman, in two chase planes, a CF-100 and a *Sabre*, had been airborne for some time, their expectant circling driving the tension and excitement ever higher. All at once the purposeful thunder of the twin Pratt & Whitney J-75's signaled Zura's initiation of the takeoff run. The gleaming white interceptor accelerated swiftly, surprisingly swiftly considering that its all-up weight exceeded that of many WW II bombers. At 120 knots Zura lifted the nosewheel, and seconds later, at 170 knots, *Arrow* 25201 lifted cleanly from the concrete and soared effortlessly skyward. Despite the great weight — the average takeoff weight in early flights was in the order of 67,000 pounds, i.e., about the weight of a fully loaded *Lancaster* — Zura lifted the *Arrow* off easily after a run of only 3,000 feet. The watchers sighed; the first great threshold had been crossed. The all-important finale — a safe landing — still had to be brought off.

After putting the aircraft through its basic paces, with every movement being carefully photographed by Woodman and Potocki from the strategically positioned chase planes, Zura swept back into the circuit. Moments later the *Arrow* was settling toward the runway on final, about to terminate its 35-minute flight. The spectators, amongst whom was Air Marshal Curtis, scarcely dared breathe. Triumph or disaster at this point might well be separated by only a few knots of airspeed and the nerve of the man alone in the cockpit. The delta wing flared gently over the runway, flashed along above it for two or three seconds, then sank gently. A puff of smoke signaled the union of tires and concrete and the *Arrow* was down, racing, nose high, along the runway.

As the nosewheel settled firmly onto the concrete Zura streamed the drag chute, and it shortly became obvious that with some positive braking he was going to have enough runway. Although it had been calculated that touchdown could normally be made at 168 knots, Zura had understandably kept several knots in hand on this first test so as to reduce the risk of an unexpected stall. His landing run was therefore fast — the *Arrow* was a fairly "hot" aircraft at optimum landing speeds — but with the aircraft's recently enlarged braking capacity this was no longer a problem[1].

Five minutes later the *Arrow* came to a stop on the apron, and Zura's exultant compatriots carried him off in triumph on their shoulders. For some time everyone around the *Arrow* was exchanging excited congratulations and posing joyously while the photographers recorded the sweet moment of success.

The great watershed had been passed: the *Arrow* had made its first flight and had fully lived up to expectations. Eight years earlier, on January 19th, 1950, Bill Waterton had given the Avro CF-100 its ten-minute virgin flight (also under the gaze of Air Marshal Curtis) and had enthusiastically predicted that it would be a great success. Now the *Arrow* promised to carry Avro into the forefront again.

To the small group of insiders watching it the *Arrow's* second flight was even more dramatic than its first. In his capacity as Supervisor of Experimental Flight Test Engineering, Fred Matthews worked closely with Zurakowski throughout the program, and maintained a close scrutiny on operations at every stage. In his correspondence Mr. Matthews began his description of the second flight by inserting a reminder of the Minneapolis-Honeywell stability augmentation system, mentioning again that "it included sensors measuring attitude changes (pitch, roll and yaw) which were interpreted by the system and translated into control signals superimposed on the aircraft controls to damp out undesirable oscillations in the aircraft attitude."

"When the *Arrow* took off, it was an awesome sight to stand at the brakes-off point and watch it accelerate down the runway and then rotate into takeoff attitude. Delta wing aircraft takeoff attitudes are typically very nose high. When viewed from the rear, you have the impression of looking down on the aircraft.

---

1. Jan Zurakowski very kindly wrote to me after the first printing of this book to clarify a point regarding the braking system. The brakes originally installed had less than half the required braking capacity. The initial taxying and braking tests thus revealed very high temperatures being transmitted to the discs and braking pads, and, of course, eventually being relayed through the rims to the tires. Since the tires were inflated to a pressure of over 250 pounds per square inch, these high temperatures would overheat them and take them close to the blowout point — often some minutes after the aircraft

"On the second flight of the first *Arrow* (25201), I was in the radio truck at the brakes-off point and watched it roll down the runway and rotate. The moment it became airborne, one wing took a sickening drop; I thought it would touch the runway, then it snapped back up and the takeoff continued.

"After the flight, it was discovered that the roll-damping sensors had been hooked up backwards by the Minneapolis-Honeywell crew. So, when there was a roll disturbance, the damping system accentuated it instead of suppressing it. Zura saved the aircraft by realizing immediately what the problem was and switching off the damping system — the switch was by his thumb on the stick. I was thankful Zura was flying. I'm not sure anyone else would have reacted in time to save the aircraft."

It is interesting to speculate as to what Zura told the ground crew following that flight. He was a quiet man, but very forceful when aroused — and he was a stickler for meticulous performance. Fred Matthews painted an intriguing portrait of him in three short paragraphs:

"All the test pilots at Avro were exceptional. Each had unique and extensive experience, a good rapport with Engineering and Flight Test Engineering, and each had a memorable personality. Of all of them, though, Zura was my favorite. His modesty was exceeded only by his ability. He was seldom, if ever, loquacious, particularly when talking on the radio. I used to joke that the wings could be falling off and he'd report when asked how he was doing . . . "fine" . . . his typical response.

"Although he didn't talk much, he usually got his message

---

had stopped. It was appreciated that if the tires burst, pieces of hard rubber hurtling about under that pressure would have lethal potentialities, so a final test was arranged to take them to their limit, simulating emergency stopping at high aircraft load. Mr. Zurakowski went on to say "We fully expected that the overheated tires would explode shortly after test. After completing the accelerated run, therefore, I stopped the aircraft at the edge of the airfield and was instructed to stay in the cockpit until I heard four explosions. Only after the explosions could the ground crew approach the aircraft.

"Before the first flight on RL 201 new brakes were fitted of satisfactory braking capacity. During the landing run I did not use the brakes hard and there were no tire explosions."

across. He would often sign the "snag" sheets, after a flight, with a simple "N N S", meaning "no new snags" . . . a subtle hint that the old snags hadn't been cleaned up.

"He was a stickler for cockpit cleanliness. There had been one or two instances of stray bolts or other lost items jamming controls. His method of checking for such items (while he was testing the *Arrow's* predecessor, the CF-100) was to fly upside down and see what ended up on the canopy. If he found anything, the groundcrew knew they were in for a chewing out because he would appear over the field upside down — just as a forewarning!"

The flight testing of the *Arrow* proceeded at a gratifying pace, partly because of the high quality of the test pilots and their aircraft, and partly because the process for analyzing the flight test results had been organized with the utmost efficiency. During the testing of the earlier CF-100, on-board recorders had been used, and in most cases observers had sat in the rear cockpit monitoring ad hoc instrumentation set up for each particular test. The *Arrow* also used on-board recorders; but on only one occasion was a rear cockpit observer carried.

Instead, for analysis of the *Arrow's* flight performance, extensive use was made of telemetry. The transmissions were received in a trailerized telemetry station where the data were fed to a real-time operations room in which engineering and flight test specialists observed the readings while the flight was actually in progress.

The on-board telemetry system and recorders were located in the large armament bay that nestled within the lower confines of the *Arrow's* fuselage. Sensors located throughout the aircraft in the various systems sent data to the telemetry system and recorders by signal wires that terminated near the armament bay in a large patch panel. This panel allowed measurements to be selected for a given flight and patched into the recorders and telemetry.

In the operations room, the information transmitted was read out primarily on strip-chart recorders. The recorders were modified so that the paper with the data recorded on it, instead of simply winding up in a roll, was drawn along a long, thin table. The experts in the various disciplines gathered round the table and scrutinzed the data as it appeared. This real-time evaluation permitted the pilot to carry on and probe further into the aircraft's flight envelope without having to land for viewing of the data before proceeding.

In addition to its telemetry readout the operations room also had radio contact with the pilot, so that the ground monitors could speak to him and get his impressions in real-time. The radio contact also permitted any desired changes in the flight plan to be transmitted direct to the pilot. Over and above the radio link there was a "hot line" telephone connection to Edgar, Ontario (near Lake Simcoe), one of the Air Defence tracking stations. Describing this adjunct of the operations facilities, Fred Matthews says:

"Zura and I had made arrangements with the Air Force for radar coverage of all flights, to aid in navigation and to give warning of any air traffic in the test air. The hot line came into our ops room. Any information they provided was transmitted from the ops room to the aircraft. Edgar was not in direct contact with the aircraft. The hot line terminated in a squawk box on the wall so that all could hear. The microphone at the Edgar radar operator's console was normally open, so we often heard radar operator conversations in the background."

This connection with the voice of the unseen Air Force radar tracker occasionally provided interesting insights into the *Arrow's* progress through the eyes of unknown third parties. On Friday, April 18th, 1958, the *Arrow* was scheduled to make a high speed run. It had already flown once that day, but shortly before 5:00 p.m. Zura took off again, this time accompanied by two chase planes. Again Spud Potocki flew a CF-100, and F/L Jack Woodman an Orenda-powered *Sabre*. Although the *Arrow* had gone supersonic before, watchers on the ground that afternoon got clear evidence of the fact that Zura had opened the throttle wider than usual. The contrails spawned by the *Arrow* during its high altitude run drew away sharply from the flanking trails of the *Sabre* and the CF-100, tracing a graphic picture of the great disparity in speeds.

Zura had been instructed to take the *Arrow* on a route high up over Tobermory (at the tip of the Bruce Peninsula between Georgian Bay and Lake Huron) and then back for a run towards Peterborough and Kingston. His flight path was designed to take him right over the Air Force radar site at Edgar. Fred Matthews was at his post in the operations room as Zura began to feed the power to the *Arrow:*

"As the aircraft accelerated past Mach 1 and started to approach Mach 2, you could hear the radar operator at Edgar muttering to himself 'Look at that son-of-a-bitch go! . . . WILL . . . YOU . . . LOOK . . . AT THAT SON OF A BITCH GO!!' He probably hadn't seen anything much faster than an F-86 before.

"I don't recall the exact speed reached (which was determined after detailed analysis of the data and corrections applied for instrument error and the like). However, the exciting part was that at the end of the run, *the aircraft was still climbing and still accelerating!* We never did find out how fast it would go, particularly with the *Iroquois*, which was never flown in an *Arrow* . . . From the data of this and other flights it was apparent that the *Arrow* was at least as good as the estimates, and probably better, although the maximum speed might have been constrained because of the structural effects of temperature. One of the things being probed in the flight test program was structural temperatures and their build-up and dissipation in the aircraft. For safety reasons, we constrained the 'gs' in the early flying after the aircraft had flown at high Mach numbers until we learned more about the heating characteristics of the aircraft."

Immediately after the speed run on April 18th, 1958, RCAF Headquarters announced, in a message marked by carefully guarded wording and understatement, that the *Arrow* had attained a speed *over* one and one-half times the speed of sound at an altitude of 50,000 feet. The official release simply pointed out that Mach 1.5 was roughly equivalent to 1,000 miles per hour, then went on to say that for security reasons it was not proposed to release any further specific performance figures as the aircraft went through its test program.

Unofficial estimates, some of them from knowledgeable sources, placed the *Arrow's* maximum speed — while still operating with the interim Pratt & Whitney J-75 P-3 power plant — at a figure close to 1400 miles per hour. While these were admittedly "guesstimates" they did not overlook the significance of those two vitally important factors associated with the April 18th run: "still *climbing* and still *accelerating*". Each of those conditions — since they had been substantial enough to record — meant that even more speed could be demonstrated in a level flight test. And a few months hence a further and much more impressive increase in speed was assured when the *Iroquois* engine became ready for installation in the Mark 2 airframe[1]. There was a distinct air of exultation in the operations room.

Excitement was occasionally generated there by less satisfying events; but the efficiency of the ops room met the challenge. Fred Matthews had assigned one of the flight test engineers, a recently retired RAF Wing Commander, to act as ops room-to-aircraft communicator. The purpose in having a specific individual, and a well qualified individual, discharge this role was primarily to ensure an orderly and systematic linkage between the aircraft and the ops room. As Matthews explains: "there is nothing more confusing than having a couple of engineering "experts" both trying to talk to the pilot at once". Matthews had also given the communicator instructions to make contingency plans covering various potential problems in flight. The former Wing Commander did his job well.

On one flight, as the *Arrow* was returning to base, a TCA *Viscount* holding an earlier position in the landing pattern landed on a short cross runway. As it approached Runway 32, the 11,050 foot main runway, its undercarriage collapsed, and the *Viscount* came to rest completely blocking the only runway at Malton capable of accommodating the *Arrow*.

The *Arrow* was at the end of its flight, hence short on fuel; and there were few runways in those days that could handle it. But the ground-to-air communicator had everything organized in a matter

---

1. The Pratt & Whitney J-75, with which the Mark I was equipped, could generate, with afterburner, approximately 18,000 lbs. of thrust — the *Iroquois*, 25,000 lbs.

of minutes. As part of his contingency planning he had listed all the available landing fields suitable for the *Arrow* (including one or two in the United States), with phone numbers, contacts, facilities and distances all set out — including the vital information of the quantity of fuel necessary to reach them.

The communicator quickly diverted the *Arrow* to Trenton, Ontario, and by the time it got there all had been made ready. Fred Matthews adds a wry commentary to this chronicle:

"While the aircraft was on its way to Trenton, the top management did not realize that we had already diverted the aircraft, and were busy contemplating the pros and cons of having the *Arrow* land at Ottawa for political reasons — i.e., an opportunity to show off the aircraft.

"There was a considerable amount of disappointment when they realized we had already diverted, and some surprise that we were so well organized and able to do it so quickly. I must say it was a bit disconcerting to us in Flight Test that they should be surprised that we were organized!"

A minor setback occurred on June 11th. As the *Arrow* approached to land, a malfunction occurred in the mechanism of the port landing gear as it was being extended. It did extend, but it failed to rotate fully and line up truly with the fore and aft axis of the aircraft. Thus on touchdown the port wheels were canted off to the left at a considerable angle. The pilot was nevertheless able to hold the aircraft on the runway for the greater part of its landing run, despite the strong pull of the tortured rubber; but towards the end the aircraft slewed and came to rest a short distance off the runway, sustaining some minor damage in the process. Following this mishap Dowty of Canada Ltd. quickly worked out a modification in the design of the undercarriage component involved, and there was no further trouble[1].

Setbacks of this type were definitely the exception rather than

---

1. Harry C. Ralph, referred to on page 33, had come from England to join A. V. Roe (in 1953) and then Dowty. In 1956 he had been obliged to return to England due to illness in the family, and was temporarily transferred back to the parent company of the Dowty Group. When the crash landing of the *Arrow* occurred on June 11th, 1958, he was on hand to provide the necessary re-design in England, as requested by A. V. Roe.

the rule at this stage of the *Arrow* program. For the most part the soundness of the design was verified by an almost unbroken string of successes in the comprehensive testing program[1].

Success was not a phenomenon restricted to Canadian military aviation. It was in this summer of 1958 that Captain Walter W. Irwin, a pilot of the 83rd Fighter Interceptor Squadron, USAF, successfully challenged the existing world speed record of 1207.6 m.p.h. in a Lockheed F-104 *Starfighter*. Taking off from Palmdale, California, Captain Irwin climbed to an altitude of approximately eight miles to make his 20-second run along the measured course, at the end of which he had advanced the world's record almost 200 m.p.h. to a new record of 1404.19 miles per hour. Twenty minutes after takeoff he was back on the ground. He had put Lockheed in the enviable position of holding three world's records: for height, 91,249 feet (also established in a *Starfighter*, only a short time earlier), for distance, 11,235.6 miles (in a *Neptune* in October, 1946) and, most important of all, for speed.

Captain Irwin's accomplishment in the *Starfighter* occasioned no disappointment at Avro. Rather, it was regarded as an event that would simply lend emphasis to the feats they knew they could expect from the *Arrow.*

Ironically, as the *Arrow's* deferred successes in the air began accumulating to impressive proportions, the program began encountering growing problems on the ground.

---

1. The stability augmentation system manifested another dangerous eccentricity well after the near mishap on the second flight described by Fred Matthews. Spud Potocki experienced unexpected problems on his landing run after completing a flight in aircraft RL 202. Again, Jan Zurakowski was good enough to write and draw this to my attention, quoting from a lecture he had delivered before the Canadian Aviation Historical Society in Toronto on March 1st, 1978:

"The second accident took place on aircraft No. 202 flown by Spud Potocki. During a landing run all four wheels skidded and the tires burst. The pilot lost directional control and the aircraft ran off the runway damaging the right undercarriage leg.

"The initial impression was that it was a pilot error. The pilot applied too much braking pressure too early and locked the wheels.

"As I mentioned before, we had the telemetry system recording basic parameters of flight. It was recorded that during touchdown the elevators suddenly moved full 30 degrees down.

" 'Spud' was sure that he did not move the controls. Instrumentation experts suspected an error in recordings.

"Fortunately, a photograph of this landing run was discovered in the possession of a suspected spy, showing that the elevators were full down. Now the cause of the

John Diefenbaker's Progressive Conservatives had not been elected at a propitious moment in the country's economic cycle. The financial burdens they involuntarily acquired through that accident of timing they proceeded to accentuate with a variety of costly new programs. Some of these, as has already been indicated, were nothing more than basic social justice, and were considerably overdue. Others had less intrinsic merit. Furthermore, like all new governments, the Conservatives had inherited a substantial number of programs from their predecessors which they were committed by the exigencies of practical politics to carry on, but which they could cheerfully have done without. The cumulative effects of these various economic determinants gave Donald Fleming, the Minister of Finance, a particularly difficult time, and stimulated a growing uneasiness in Cabinet over the rising cost of the *Arrow* program — a program which already had the disadvantage of being a legacy from the St. Laurent government.

C. D. Howe's original estimate of $100 million for the *Arrow's* development was already clearly identifiable as a gross miscalculation. At the end of fiscal year 1957-58 it had already cost $235

---

accident was clear. The *Arrow's* elevators were large and when deflected fully down acted as powerful flaps, increasing wing lift so much that only 20 percent of the aircraft weight was on the main wheels. The pilot was not aware of this and normal application of brakes locked the wheels.

"During this landing a small aircraft vibration as the wheels touched the ground resulted in a wrong electrical signal to the stability augmentation system calling for full elevator down.

"The pilot was lucky: if the elevator moved fully down in flight at any speed faster than 300 knots, disintegration of the aircraft was likely in a fraction of a second!"

million, and it appeared that well over another $100 million would be required for the fiscal year 1958-59. The chronology of the account — and the estimate at the beginning of 1958 — looked like this:

1954-55:	$ 17,000,000
1955-56:	38,000,000
1956-57:	65,000,000
1957-58:	115,000,000
1958-59:	100,000,000
	$335,000,000

Bearing in mind that the *Arrow* program was only one program, albeit the most costly one in the Department of National Defence, the government now began to watch it even more critically than before despite the lengthening record of success in the *Arrow's* air trials.

In the Chiefs of Staff Committee the tide was beginning to run against the *Arrow*. Air Marshal Hugh Campbell, who had succeeded Air Marshal Slemon as Chief of Air Staff in 1957, faced a group of service peers who were understandably growing more and more reluctant to see the basic requirements of their own services cut each year so as to ensure the continuance of funding for the *Arrow*. In 1955 Lieutenant-General Guy Simonds had resigned his post as the Army's Chief of Staff and taken early retirement, partially because the Liberal government would not accept his recommendation that some measure of compulsory selective service be implemented in peacetime, and partially in protest against the continued funding of the *Arrow*. After the 1958 election, when the new administration's support for the *Arrow* was sensed to be no more than lukewarm, Air Marshal Campbell's position vis-à-vis the other Chiefs became more difficult.

The Chairman of the Chiefs of Staff Committee was an Army man, General Charles Foulkes. The Army's Chief of Staff was General Graham and the Navy's Admiral Mainguy. The other voting member of the Committee was Dr. Solandt of the Defence Research

Board. The Deputy Minister of National Defence, Frank Miller, while not a voting member, was always invited to attend the Committee's meetings — and as a matter of practice always accepted. The Secretary of the Cabinet, Gordon Robertson, was always invited, as was the Under Secretary of State for External Affairs, Jules Leger. Cabinet was clearly in a position to be kept fully aware of every nuance of the positions taken by the various Chiefs on matters of defence policy. Certainly the Minister of National Defence, with his own Deputy attending every meeting, was kept abreast of all business on the Chiefs' agenda, and could have a summary of the points expressed by everyone participating.

From a reading of the Hansards covering a later period one concludes that after *Sputnik* had been launched the Chiefs had been prompted, as one would expect, to review the *Arrow's* role and its usefulness. Other information they considered germane appears to be that, apart from *Sputnik's* demonstration of a significant advance in Russia's offensive potential, the Russian bomber types known by the code names *Bear* and *Bison* were the most advanced that the Russians seemed interested in producing; and those were the only two types of Soviet bomber that could reach North America from Russia and return to their bases. Thus, coupled with the Russians' premature advance in missile capability was the fact that their bomber threat was materializing more slowly, and in more limited dimensions, than foreseen. These, at least, are the *ex post facto* gleanings of the Canadian Chiefs' conclusions that one would reconstruct from Hansard and other reported speeches of members of the government.

But although no mention is made of them, one is forced to conclude that other significant facts must have been brought forward and examined, since the discussions going on contemporaneously in the United States had a noticeably different complexion in this area of the bomber threat. Even that portion of the American discussions that was made public makes this clear; and certainly the Canadian Chiefs would be privy, through their NORAD and NATO links, with much else besides. One gathers that in the United States General Twining, General White (Chief of Staff, USAF) and other senior

American airmen were expressing their considered view that Russia would likely proceed with the development of a bomber having greatly superior performance to the *Bear* and the *Bison*.

Nevertheless there was no public mention made of this likelihood by the Canadian government, and it is difficult to understand the omission. What is clear is that during the summer of 1958 Mr. Diefenbaker's attitude toward the *Arrow* turned distinctly hostile — in the face of exemplary progress in the air testing and production of the machine.

On this latter point it should be mentioned that for the purpose of speeding full production, whenever that step was finally authorized, Avro had taken a great gamble and gone straight to a production line form of operation in turning out the first models of the *Arrow*. Normally a builder will proceed with one or more prototypes, virtually hand-built models, iron out the bugs with custom tailored modifications, then set up a production line geared to turn out the final version as proved by the flight testing program.

Gambling on the validity of their intensive wind tunnel testing, Avro's management had gone directly to production line construction. If a serious flaw in design had been revealed in the flight testing program, something entailing substantial modification of the aircraft, this could have resulted in formidable expense and considerable delay. But the testing uncovered no such error; rather, it rapidly verified the soundness of the design and established the great potential of the basic airframe. Thus the first machines, although frequently referred to as prototypes, were not prototypes in the normal sense; they were basically production line aircraft. In spite of the delays caused by factors beyond their control — such as delays occasioned through requiring Canadian suppliers to build to much higher specifications than they had been accustomed to, and the time wasted as a result of the abandonment by British and American engine manufacturers of two different power plants chosen for the *Arrow* — the company had recovered much lost ground by its own initiative. Its boldness and enterprise were not to be rewarded.

On September 23rd, 1958, the Prime Minister issued a chilling press release in which he said:

"The government has concluded that missiles should be introduced into the Canadian air defence system and that the number of supersonic interceptor aircraft required for the RCAF air defence command will be substantially less than could have been foreseen a few years ago, *if in fact such aircraft will be required at all in the 1960's* in view of the rapid strides being made in missiles by both the United States and the U.S.S.R. [author's italics.] The development of the Canadian supersonic interceptor aircraft, the CF-105 or the *"Arrow"*, was commenced in 1953 and even under the best of circumstances it will not be available for effective use in squadrons until late in 1961. Since the project began, revolutionary changes have taken place which have made necessary a review of the program in the light of anticipated conditions when the aircraft comes into use. The preponderance of expert opinion is that by the 1960's manned aircraft, however outstanding, will be less effective in meeting the threat than previously expected.

". . . The government believes, however, that to discontinue abruptly the development of this aircraft and its engine, with its consequent effects upon the industry, would not be prudent with the international outlook as uncertain and tense as it is. As a measure of insurance, with present tensions as they are, therefore the government has decided that the development program for the *Arrow* aircraft and *Iroquois* engine should be continued until next March, when the situation will be reviewed again in the light of all the existing circumstances at that time."

This portion of the statement laid much stress on someone's perception of the implications of changing tactical and strategic factors; but a later passage reflected the Prime Minister's overriding concern with the economics of the situation when he said that he recognized the accomplishments and the technical quality of the work done, but that to continue "vast expenditures on aircraft and equipment which military and other expert opinion does not support . . . would not only be wasteful but unjustifiable".

While the Prime Minister's statement had clearly ominous overtones so far as the long-term future of the *Arrow* program was concerned, it was highly indefinite to say the least. It had been fashioned by a cautious hand, leaving Mr. Diefenbaker a comfortable supply of loopholes and ambiguities which he could cite selectively and with infinite variations of emphasis to soothe challengers of whatever stripe. The company recognized the speech's motivating concern as economic[1], and indeed thoughtful Canadians everywhere had reason to review the economics of the government's situation over-all, not just the segment relating to National Defence. The budget statement of the Diefenbaker administration on December 6th, 1957, had predicted a surplus of $152 million. In fact there was a deficit of $39 million. The 1958 federal budget, tabled by the Minister of Finance on June 17th, 1958, predicted a deficit of $648 million — the largest deficit since the end of World War II. The debatable logic of the government's vast debt roll-over, the so-called Conversion Loan of 1958, was causing some anxiety in the financial community, and no sooner had the subscription books been closed on that loan (a week before the Prime Minister's September 23rd statement) then a selling wave materialized, and the price of the bonds started into a protracted slide.

This worrying economic situation had prompted earlier vague expressions of concern regarding the *Arrow* and *Iroquois* development programs from a variety of government sources. There had been so many of these expressions, public and semi-public, that in June, 1958, Charles Grinyer had gone to Mr. O'Hurley, the Minister of Defence Production, and protested. He pointed out that he could not organize and keep intact highly skilled design and testing teams if government spokesmen were going to go out of their way to taint the air with uncertainty. Mr. O'Hurley assured him that he could ignore all the doom and gloom pronouncements — the aircraft and engine would go into production. Mr. Grinyer returned

---

1. Mr. Fred Smye, whose official title was Chief Executive Officer, Avro and Orenda, says: "In early September, 1958, I recommended to the government (Fleming, O'Hurley and Pearkes) that they should switch the fire control system and missile if they were interested in saving $350,000,000. The answer was reflected in the P.M.'s statement of September 23rd."

to his plant and spread the word. He was satisfied that O'Hurley was sincere — and to this day remains convinced that O'Hurley genuinely believed that they were going into production.

In retrospect one is constrained to say that the government had been given every reason to be satisfied with progress on the *Iroquois* engine development program. In 1957 the president of Curtiss-Wright had been so impressed with the engine's performance and potential that he had journeyed to Orenda's plant at Malton and signed a seven-year contract. Under its terms Curtiss-Wright would be entitled to build the *Iroquois* under licence in the United States. He had been candid enough to state publicly that the Orenda *Iroquois* was several years ahead of any engine then under development in the United States — and coming from the president of one of the Big Three this was certainly a ringing endorsement of the calibre of the Canadian power plant. Under a proviso of the contract, Curtiss-Wright would not be bound until the engine had actually passed its Official Type Test; but it was obvious that Curtiss-Wright were familiar enough with current progress, and with Charles Grinyer's past accomplishments, to realize that at this stage passing the Type Test under the aegis of Charles Grinyer was as good as done. After the contract was signed there was speculation that the *Iroquois* might be used eventually to power the North American F-108, which was still a long way from completion.

Having secured Mr. O'Hurley's reassurance in June, 1958, Mr. Grinyer returned to Malton where Orenda was in the process of completing a new $6,500,000 high altitude test cell facility under the immediate direction of P. K. Peterson, the Chief Equipment Engineer. The new test cell was capable of providing a flight operating range, for an *Iroquois* under test, from Mach 1.3 at 35,000 feet to Mach 2.9 at 100,000 feet. The construction of the Malton cell marked one stage in an $11,000,000 program begun three years earlier with financial assistance from the Department of National Defence[1].

The September 23rd press conference called by the Prime

---

1. "Canadian Aviation", issue of March, 1959, pp 30-33.

Minister came as another unexpected blow to Charles Grinyer after the commitments given him by Mr. O'Hurley. Nevertheless, he carried on, and managed to keep things in the plant on an even keel until, a few weeks later, the October 25th, 1958, issue of Macleans hit the newsstands. This issue contained a truly remarkable article by Maclean's Ottawa Editor, Blair Fraser. It was remarkable in its merciless criticism of the *Arrow* program, in its eager interpretation of the September 23rd speech as the certain death knell of the whole project, and in its support of the Prime Minister in a "ready-aye-ready" stance. This latter feature was perhaps the most surprising aspect of the whole article.

Blair Fraser was a dyed-in-the-wool MacKenzie King Liberal who was moved to support a Conservative policy or politician with approximately the same frequency as the visitations of Halley's comet. Fraser had never served in the armed forces himself (he was 30 years of age in 1939), having spent the years of World War II in Montreal and Ottawa writing about it. Nevertheless, in this October article he unhesitatingly delivered himself of dogmatic pronounce- ments on difficult questions of continental defence that were still dividing the counsels of Canada's professional service experts. (Fraser's heraldic pronouncements have been totally disproved by subsequent events.) Clearly aligning himself with unnamed advisers "who say the manned aircraft is as dead as the muzzle-loading musket", Fraser proceeded to smite the proponents of the *Arrow* hip and thigh, with an abundance of malice aforethought.

His article was an effectively written piece, compounded of roughly equal portions of fact, distortions of fact, gross error and half truth. Showered largely upon a relatively uninformed segment of the public, who were neither equipped nor disposed to challenge it, the article was a heavy blow. From its first paragraph it portrayed the Prime Minister as almost revelling in a Jack-the-Giant-killer role, directing his energies against hidebound aero-industry Establishment and RCAF fatcats of the Colonel Blimp mentality, struggling to launch an aircraft already a museum piece akin to the *Spitfire*. This was the opening sentence of Fraser's spiteful diatribe:

"NEVER, not even in June, 1957, has Prime Minister

Diefenbaker met the press with such well-earned glee as when he announced the discontinuance of our all-Canadian supersonic fighter aircraft, the Avro *Arrow.*"

The fact that nine months earlier the Minister primarily responsible for these matters had been quoted in the Calgary Herald as flatly contradicting allegations of the *Arrow's* imminent obsolescence did not prompt Blair Fraser to qualify his own confident assessment. On January 18th, the Herald had attributed this statement to Mr. Pearkes: "I do not share the opinion that the *Arrow* will be obsolete before it is operational. When Russia stops building bombers it will be time for us to start thinking of some other defence." Not surprisingly, that scrap of sturdy logic has stood the test of time and remains true today. But Blair Fraser was a journalist of considerable reputation, and deservedly so, for, his pronounced political asymmetry apart, he was a well educated and gifted writer. He had a wide following; and an editorial blast like his October 25th offering could be counted upon to mold a lot of opinions. It also had one result that undoubtedly never occurred to him.

Charles Grinyer tendered his resignation to the company, reluctantly concluding that he could no longer serve any useful purpose in an atmosphere that was becoming poisoned with ill-informed criticism and growing uncertainty. The shock waves of his announcement were immediate. No sooner had he heard the bad news than Mr. O'Hurley was on the telephone pressing Mr. Grinyer to withdraw his resignation and carry the *Iroquois* program to completion. Mr. Grinyer in turn re-stated the points he had made four months earlier: he simply could not expect to keep men of the calibre he had been able to attract to Malton working together on projects that looked as though they were going to be flushed down the drain. Once again Mr. O'Hurley pacified him, repeating his statements that the work was not going to be wasted, that the projects were going ahead. At his repeated request Mr. Grinyer finally agreed to withdraw his resignation, and once again relayed Mr. O'Hurley's unequivocal assurances to his senior people. It would have quieted some other people's concerns had he been able to speak in some public forum.

A number of editors accepted uncritically Mr. Diefenbaker's negatively slanted assessment of the situation on September 23rd, 1958; some even praised his government's self-discipline in thus inclining toward a decision that would be as unpalatable as it would be politically unrewarding in the several constituencies that would be directly affected. But a great many other people treated the situation to a more penetrating analysis and were seriously concerned about the portents. One well-known personage who privately expressed his deep concern at the time was John Bracken, former Premier of Manitoba, and a former National Leader of the Conservative Party.

John Bracken's concern was for the decision-making process that would be involved in the final determination of the *Arrow's* future. He felt a growing apprehension that the final decision would not be based upon a balanced consideration of all the germane factors. He was worried over the fact that many politicians seemed not to know whether there was a genuine need for the aircraft, and that few had any real appreciation of the *Arrow's* potential. He perceived that many were either unconcerned about, or, more likely, completely unaware of, the long-range economic impact of having to buy foreign aircraft in lieu of Canadian produced equipment if the domestic capability went unsupported. Privately Mr. Bracken expressed his deep concern over the all too obvious lack of a visible and persuasive champion of the *Arrow* program to present its case in its proper light, particularly the economics of the project and the alternatives available. What was required, he realized, was a knowledgeable spokesman, of stature, whose command of a national audience would ensure a fair and impartial appraisal of defence requirements, a man who could summarize with clarity what those defence needs were, the *Arrow's* role in that context, and its ability to discharge that role effectively. He was keenly aware that those RCAF officers privy to the facts were convinced that the Force would never have obtained the CF-100, one of the most efficient aircraft it ever flew, had it not been for a staunch and capable champion in the person of Air Marshal W. A. Curtis. In light of subsequent events the apprehension Mr. Bracken expressed to his confidants was not without considerable significance.

But the uncertainty and disappointment generated at Avro and Orenda Engines by the September 23rd press release and the Macleans' article of October 25th now began to dissipate in the wake of some positive acts that dispelled much of the temporary fog of bewilderment. Mr. O'Hurley's assurances were known to management, of course; but other events, which were public knowledge, were more important in this regard.

Under the pressure of the Prime Minister's clear concern over the economics of the *Arrow*, government representatives approached Crawford Gordon at A. V. Roe with the request that his people re-assess the whole *Arrow* program, take whatever drastic steps were necessary, and come up with his rock-bottom unit price for 100 *Arrows*. The major steps were very obvious at A. V. Roe; they simply involved doing what the company had recommended from the outset, namely, abandoning the development of the ASTRA weapons system and the *Sparrow II* missile and going with the "off the shelf" Hughes MX-1179 weapons system complemented by *Falcon* missiles. The RCAF were reconciled to the reversion to the Hughes system at this stage, the development of ASTRA having proved more difficult and much more expensive than originally contemplated. (Its ultimate cost had begun to look like something between 100 million and 200 million dollars.)

The company now calculated that with the switch to the Hughes MX-1179 and the *Falcon* missile they could offer the Diefenbaker administration a flyaway cost of 3.75 million dollars per aircraft. When the total number of aircraft required was reduced to 100, that meant a figure of $375,000,000, but there were other costs entailed in the full package: support spares and equipment would amount to $98,400,000; missiles would amount to $42,600,000; and the completion of the full development program on 20 aircraft (eight of which would be operational) would cost another $295,000,000. Thus the government was looking at a grand total of $781,000,000 for 100 aircraft including all the development costs and a supply of weapons and spares. (This figure was arrived at by deducting from the first figure of $375,000,000 the cost of the eight operational aircraft included in the development program.)

Work continued at Avro Aircraft and Orenda Engines in a cheerier atmosphere, and an even stronger current of optimism was stirred on November 24th, 1958, when the Deputy Commander of NORAD, Air Marshal Roy Slemon, with General Earle Partridge, the Commander, standing beside him, issued a public statement at Colorado Springs. It went a long way toward correcting misconceptions propagated in Blair Fraser's article, and was even interpreted in some quarters as a NORAD correction of possible misunderstandings engendered by the Prime Minister's September 23rd press release. The editor of the Canadian magazine "Aircraft" made careful notes of Air Marshal Slemon's statement.

In a subsequent editorial he reiterated the points made: That NORAD considered the manned interceptor a requirement for as far ahead as it was possible to see; and that an item by item comparison of the *Arrow* with other types of aircraft available within the same period, designed for a similar purpose, showed that the *Arrow* would be the highest performing interceptor available until the advent of the North American F-108. From his notes the editor quoted Air Marshal Slemon directly as follows:

"For as long as we can see we must have manned interceptors and missiles to meet the manned bomber threat.

"What sort of manned interceptor? Particularly in the fringe areas . . . experience shows the long-range interceptor with two men on board can best do the job. Why two men? Two men can best cope with the long-range navigation, interception problems, ECM operations . . . What aircraft come near this? The F-106 is a first class all-weather interceptor. The majority [built] will be single seaters, single engine."

The editor then continued: "Pointing out that it was very difficult to make direct comparison, as the peak performance of an interceptor depended on the role for which it was designed, A/M Slemon then went on to say that the CF-105 'generally speaking, will have an edge in speed, altitude, range and maneuverability over the single seat F-106, and an even greater edge over the two seater version' "[1].

These widely publicized statements went unchallenged and uncontradicted by the government. The fact was that the government was hardly in a position to challenge them, even if it had chosen to. Only four months earlier the Minister of National Defence himself had been recorded in the minutes of a meeting of the Committee on Estimates as saying (July 4th, 1958):

"For several years at least after the introduction of the ICBM the manned bomber will be an effective means of delivering attack with the degree of accuracy required . . .

"There are important factors necessitating the use of manned interceptors in the air defence system for many years; indeed, as far as we can see into the future . . .

"The supersonic manned interceptor is the development of a proven weapon, whereas the long-range surface-to-air missile is as yet untried."

Far from attempting to explain away or distinguish his earlier statement, George Pearkes stuck to his guns, called a press conference himself on November 25th, the day following Air Marshal Slemon's pronouncement, and confirmed the point that the RCAF would require a manned interceptor for some years to come. He was also quoted in the press as having amplified this statement in a reference to the September 23rd press release in which he said: "What we decided last September was not to produce the *Arrow* under the conditions that surrounded *Arrow* production at that time. Let the makers re-examine the cost and then we will know where we are going." This exercise, of course, the manufacturers were in the process of completing, as a result of which the flyaway price per unit of 3.75 million dollars was determined.

These authoritative public pronouncements were instrumental in elevating morale at Avro and Orenda. The only thing that could have increased confidence still further would have been an announcement that George Pearkes had finally been successful in his continuing quest for another NATO government willing to buy the

---

1. "Aircraft", December, 1958 issue, p 90.

Arrow. But it was common knowledge that he was engaged in an up-hill fight. He had gone to Washington a few months earlier, in the summer of 1958, to deal personally with the American Secretary for Defence, Mr. McElroy. As Mr. Pearkes subsequently explained: "I did my best to interest him in this aircraft . . . then, when we were attending the NATO conference in Paris we did our best once again to interest the United States in the program of the CF-105. Mr. McElroy was there on that occasion together with Mr. Dulles and other representatives of the United States . . . We were told definitely and with finality that the United States could not include the CF-105 in its armament inventory." In fact the United States' government attitude had been hardening for many months, as was evidenced by the UPI despatch carried in the Toronto Telegram as early as June 16th, 1958:

"United States defence officials said today the main reason for the continued refusal of the United States to buy Canada's Avro CF-105 fighter plane is that the *Arrow* cannot fly at top speed long enough.

"The *Arrow* is capable of speeds above 2,000 miles an hour only in short bursts.

"The officials said further that the United States could hardly buy the *Arrow* from Canada when it has suspended production at home of two very similar aircraft."

Mr. Pearkes did not give up easily; as he later pointed out, he had taken the matter up with the Minister of Defence of the United Kingdom. He pursued the matter diligently until the middle of February, 1959, at which point he received a telegram stating very definitely that the U.K. government would not be able to consider the purchase of the CF-105.

Apart from the reason stated above, it was obvious that the United States government would be less than enthusiastic about the *Arrow*, not because it did not live up to its projected performance, but for the much more practical reason that Lockheed was busily developing variants of the F-104 *Starfighter*, McDonnell was developing the F-101 *Voodoo*, and the F-106 and F-108 were under development. Any realist would understand that the American government would be subject to strong pressure to put its taxpayers' money into American-built aircraft. And, no less than Air Marshal Curtis, the American Chiefs of Staff would realize the potentially prejudicial consequences of being dependent upon a source of supply north of the border for such an important weapon. They had never bought the CF-100 from Canada, despite its admitted excellence and their frequently repeated adjurations that the NATO partners should standardize upon the best weapons and buy from one another, rather than buying domestic products of less than top calibre. Nevertheless, while it was obvious that they could not be expected to have all their interceptor aircraft built in Canada and subject to the vagaries of Canadian politics, it remained quite within the realm of possibility, bearing in mind the size of their own domestic aircraft industry, that they could at least have purchased a limited number of CF-100s or CF-105 *Arrows*, or built them under license in American factories. George Pearkes, V.C., did his best; and Canada could hardly have sent a representative with better credentials or a better product — at least a better product on paper.

That the attitude of the United States had cooled and hardened was due in part to a factor which had nothing to do with strategic considerations — at least this is the firm opinion of a number of senior Canadian officials who were close to the events. This extraneous factor was Mr. Diefenbaker himself — and his policies.

John Diefenbaker made it clear from the outset that he was definitely not pro-American. He appointed some Ministers with a similar or even stronger bent, and none of them were at pains to disguise their sentiments. Those sentiments might more fairly have been described as energetically pro-British rather than anti-American, although at a later stage the anti-American animus was patent.

The earliest manifestation of these feelings had occurred in the summer of 1957 when Mr. Diefenbaker proposed to divert no less than fifteen per cent of Canada's imports from America to the United Kingdom. He reiterated this proposal on a number of occasions, and at least once coupled it with a vague justification that hinted at the economic hazard implicit in Canada's existing trade pattern, linked arterially as it was with the American economy.

There were other straws in the wind as well, and they did not go unnoticed by the American government. By the beginning of 1959, the co-operative ardour of senior American officials, who had hitherto gone out of their way to assist with the development of the *Arrow* and the *Iroquois* engine, cooled noticeably. The Diefenbaker government seemed unaware of the fact that it requires much charm to retain friends while you amuse yourself by poking them in the eye. But at year-end, 1958, the climate of inter-governmental relationships was not at the forefront of anyone's consciousness at Avro or Orenda. Everyone was too busy.

Apart from installing telemetry equipment on *Arrows* six, seven and eight, the Avro workers were proceeding as quickly as possible with the structural modifications that the *Arrows* would require to accommodate the Hughes weapons system. Air Vice-Marshal John Easton, as Air Member for Technical Services, had negotiated the loan of MX-1179 weapons systems from the USAF, and after the cancellation of the ASTRA-*Sparrow* programs, Avro had been granted a new contract in November covering the installation of the American weapons system and the design changes this would entail as a prerequisite.

Under the spur of government requests to speed delivery dates December and January were marked by feverish activity on the *Arrow* production line. By February five fully completed and airworthy *Arrows* were in existence — one of which had been briefly sidelined by the landing accident of June 11th, 1958 — and February was ushered in at Avro in the exhilarating knowledge that in a few short weeks *Arrow* Number 6 would be ready. Over *Arrow* Number 6 great expectations hovered. Number 6 was the first of the Mark II's, the first *Arrow* equipped with Orenda's tailor-made *Iroquois* engine; and the *Iroquois* PS-13 promised to send the *Arrow* through the air at unheard of speeds. The first *Arrow* had been equipped with a J-75 P3 engine and its four Mark I successors had each carried a J-75 P5, an engine with a "dry" thrust of 12,500 pounds which could generate 18,500 pounds of thrust with its afterburners.

The brand new *Iroquois* was designed to produce 20,000 pounds of dry thrust, of course — a remarkable 54 per cent increase

— and 25,000 pounds of thrust with afterburner augmentation, the latter representing a 40.54 per cent increase over the J-75's power with afterburner.

Everyone at Avro realized that the Mark I could probably set a new world's speed record itself if given the assignment. So what would *Arrow* Number 6 do, with a full 40 per cent increase in power? In addition, it was noted, *Arrow* Number 6 with the *Iroquois* engine would have that large increase in power applied to a lighter aircraft; for not only were the pairs of J-75s in the first *Arrows* heavier than the *Iroquois* engines, the use of J-75s in the aircraft, originally designed for another power plant, had in turn necessitated the use of nose ballast to maintain the centre of gravity at the appropriate point. (In high performance aircraft particularly, a shift in c.g. of only a few inches can precipitate acute and dangerous handling problems.)

With the great increase in thrust, coupled to a reduction of 4,000 - 5,000 pounds in all-up weight, a radical increase in speed was guaranteed for the Mark II *Arrow*. Complementing this greatly enhanced performance, the plans for succeeding Marks of the *Arrow* called for the installation of extra fuel tanks for longer range. All in all, the aircraft's capabilities were so outstanding that, in the minds of the Avro and Orenda work force there could be no question of holding back on full production once Number 6 was sent aloft. This conclusion could only be reinforced by the reasoning that a nation that had spent $341,000,000 to bring itself to the very threshold of full production of what promised to be the finest interceptor aircraft in the world for several years (until the F-108 was ready) was not likely to cast its advantage away. Furthermore, apart from the production contract, which was all the September 23rd press release had deferred judgement on, Avro had separate contracts on an initial group of 37 aircraft, and contracts that called for advanced research and test programs on approximately 20 of those. None of these development and research contracts had been called into question; and behind the scenes Mr. Grinyer and other company officials had been given the private reassurances referred to. February 20th, 1959, rolled around.

Chapter 9

On Friday, February 20th, 1959, at 11:00 a.m., Prime Minister Diefenbaker rose at the opening of the House of Commons and spoke to a suddenly hushed audience:

"Mr. Speaker, with the leave of the house I should like to make a somewhat lengthy statement on the subject of one facet of the national defence of Canada because, after all, the effectiveness or otherwise of the measures taken for national defence until international peace under law is obtained constitutes the passport either to survival or destruction. The announcement I wish to make has to do with the decision regarding our air defence which was foreshadowed in the statement made by me to the press on September 23 last.

"The government has carefully examined and re-examined the probable need for the *Arrow* aircraft and *Iroquois* engine known as the CF-105, the development of which has been continued pending a final decision. It has made a thorough examination in the light of all the information available concerning the probable nature of the threats to North America in future years, the alternative means of defence against such

Above: *The Arrow aloft on its first flight, photographed from a chase plane,
March 25th, 1958. The undercarriage was not retracted on this flight.*
(AIR AND SPACE DIVISION, NATIONAL MUSEUM, OTTAWA)

Below: *The critical first landing: everything hinges on Jan Zurakowski, a
talented test pilot. Zurakowski's helmet is visible in this shot as he begins his
flareout perfectly positioned over the end of the runway.*
(CAF)

Above: *Jan Zurakowski, having successfully completed the momentous first flight of the Arrow, is carried off by his exulting co-workers. On the left and right of "Zura", each holding a leg, are Peter Martin of the Project Office (wearing the short-length coat) and Derek Woolley, Flight Test Engineer (in suit). Immediately right of Derek Woolley, wearing a dark suit and clutching Zura's left ankle, is Stan Brown, Electrical Systems Design Engineer. To the right of Brown, with his left hand gripping someone else's shoulder, the wavy-haired gentleman, is Frank Chalmers, Flight Test Engineer. The balding gentleman holding a clipboard is another Flight Test Engineer, as are the two gentlemen on the extreme right of the picture, Red Warren (wearing the fur-collared jump suit) and Gordon Essilman. On the left side of the picture, the gentleman in the dark coat standing between the man with the binoculars on his chest and the man with a toque on his head is Stan Harper, Chief of Experimental Testing (Ground Test and Flight Test). Standing in this group, but not visible in this picture, was the gentleman who made all these identifications, Fred C. Matthews, Supervisor of Experimental Flight Testing.*

(AVIATION AND SPACE DIVISION, NATIONAL MUSEUM, CANADA)

t: Still receiving congratulations *his momentous test flight, Jan* *kowski is here shaking hands* *Pete Cope, Experimental Test* *.*
(AVIATION AND SPACE DIVISION, NATIONAL MUSEUM, CANADA)

w: Jack Woodman, a Flight *tenant in the RCAF, flying the* *e chase plane. Note the camera* *nted on Woodman's helmet, with* *h he photographed the Arrow at* *y salient point in its early fllights.* *dman flew on operations as a* *er in World War II and took his* *'s training in 1949. He was the* *RCAF pilot to fly the Arrow,* *ng previously been a member of* *team evaluating the F-102 for the* *ed States Air Force. Jack Wood-* *is presently Director of Flying* *rations for Lockheed Aircraft,* *lives in Palmdale, California.*
(CAF)

99

Above: *Servicing the Arrow after a test flight. Ease of maintenance had been an important objective in the design of the Arrow.*   (CAF)

Below: *Arrow No. 1 split seconds from touchdown. The pilot's visibility from the Arrow was good, even in the nose-up attitude prevailing on touchdown.*
(CAF)

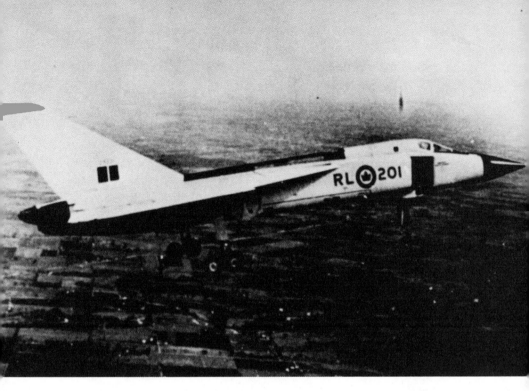

Above: *Undercarriage down, the Arrow prepares to join the circuit at Malton.*
(AIR AND SPACE DIVISION, NATIONAL MUSEUM, OTTAWA)

Below: *Arrow No. 1 is towed into the hangar past several CF-100s.* (CAF)

Above: *Gear up! '201 gets airborne from Malton. To fit into the thin wing the main undercarriage had to both shorten and rotate as it retracted.*

Below: *'202 with its drag chute streamed concludes another test flight.*

(Via P J. BRENNAN)

Above: The slight angle on the elevators and the light puff of smoke betoken a nice touchdown as the test pilot greases the Arrow on again.   (CAF)

Below: Arrow No. 2 banks slightly away above the chase plane with speed brakes extended preparatory to lowering the undercarriage. The leading edge notches are particularly noticeable in the strong sunlight.   (CAF)

On June 11, 1958 the Arrow suffered its first major accident. The left main undercarriage extended but due to a jammed chain in the rotation mechanism it failed to assume the correct fore and aft alignment (above). The result was a tremendous drag on the left side as the tires were torn to shreds (above right). The aircraft veered off the runway (right) kicking up a shower of debris. Moments later the undercarriage collapsed and the aircraft came to a halt on its belly. Damage was fortunately not severe and the aircraft was made airworthy again within a couple of months.

(Via P. J. BRENNAN)

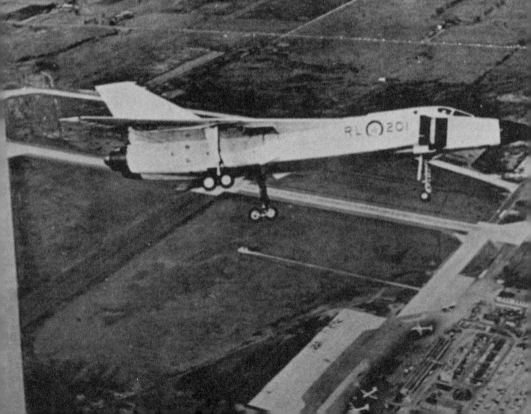

Above left: *Poetry in motion: the Arrow, "clean", cleaves the air above a backdrop of sun-touched cumulus. Its future as the leading fighter of the western world during the years until the arrival of the USAF's F-108 seemed assured at this point.*
(AIR AND SPACE DIVISION, NATIONAL MUSEUM, OTTAWA)

Below left: *Arrow No. 1 turns crosswind and prepares for the downwind leg parallel to the main runway.*
(CAF)

Above: *Arrow No. 1 streams the drag chute on its landing run. The stresses imposed by deployment of the chute were found to be considerably higher than had first been calculated, necessitating some minor modification.*
(CAF)

Below: *Arrow No. 1 heads to the hangar for another detailed inspection after test flying.*
(CAF)

Above: Arrow No. 2 flares for touchdown. (CAF)

Below: 202 leaves the characteristic trail of smoke at touchdown. (CAF)

Above: *Arrow No. 4, standing beside a CF-100, shows the great disparity in size and height between the two aircraft. Note the dayglo-orange markings on the nose, spine and vertical tail.* (AIR AND SPACE DIVISION, NATIONAL MUSEUM, OTTAWA)

Below: *An aerial view of the Avro Aircraft hangars at Malton.* (CAF)

Above: *Another good view of the Arrow "clean".* (CAF)

Below: *Arrow No. 4 in front of the hangar at Malton with the crew access ladder in place. Note that both canopies are open.* (T. STACHIW)

Above: *This view emphasizes the dart-like configuration of the aircraft.*

(T. STACHIW)

Below: *This aspect tends to disguise the aircraft's size.*

(T. STACHIW)

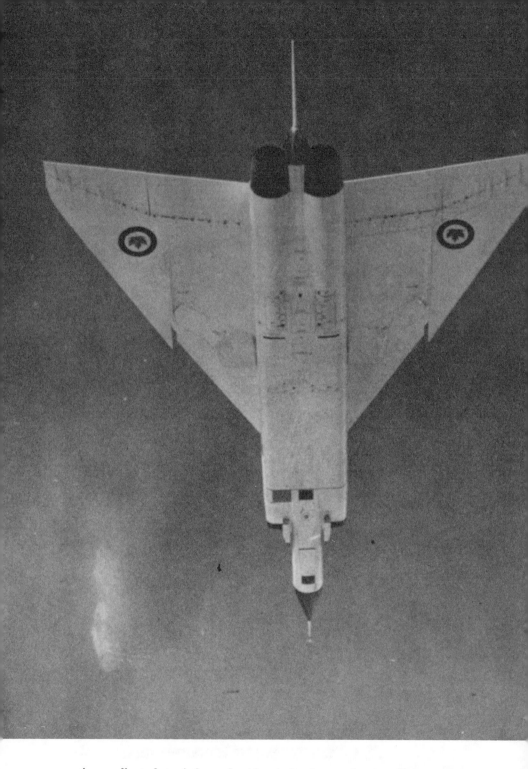

An excellent shot of the underside of the Arrow showing the numerous inspection panels and the angularity of the fuselage lines. (Via P. J. BRENNAN)

threats, and the estimated costs thereof. The conclusion arrived at is that the development of the *Arrow* aircraft and *Iroquois* engine should be terminated now.

"Formal notice of termination is being given now to the contractors. All outstanding commitments will of course be settled equitably.

"In reaching this decision the government has taken fully into account the present and prospective international situation, including the strategic consequences of weapon development and the effects of the decision I have just announced upon Canada's ability to meet any emergency that may arise.

"Work on the original concept of the CF-105 commenced in the air force in 1952, and the first government decision to proceed with the development and with the production of two prototypes was taken late in 1953. The plane was designed to meet the requirements of the RCAF for a successor to the CF-100 to be used in the defence of Canada. At that time it was thought some five or six hundred aircraft would be needed by the RCAF, and their cost was forecast at about $1,500,000 to $2 million each.

"From the beginning, however, it was recognized by the previous government, and subsequently by this government, that the development of an advanced supersonic aircraft such as the 105 and its complicated engine and weapon system was highly hazardous, and therefore all decisions to proceed with it were tentative and subject to change in the light of experience. This was known to the contractors undertaking the development, to the air force, and to parliament.

"The development of the *Arrow* aircraft and the *Iroquois* engine has been a success although, for various reasons, it has been much behind the original schedule. The plane and its engine have shown promise of achieving the high standard of technical performance intended, and are a credit to those who conceived and designed them and translated the plans into reality.

"Unfortunately these outstanding achievements have been

overtaken by events. In recent months it has come to be realized that the bomber threat against which the CF-105 was intended to provide defence has diminished, and alternative means of meeting the threat have been developed much earlier than was expected.

"The first modern long range bombers with which Canada might be confronted came into operation over five years ago, but the numbers produced now appear to be much lower than was previously forecast. Thus the threat against which the CF-105 could be effective has not proved to be as serious as was forecast. During 1959 and 1960 a relatively small number of modern bombers constitutes the main airborne threat. It is considered that the defence system of North America is adequate to meet this threat.

"Potential aggressors now seem more likely to put their effort into missile development than into increasing their bomber force. By the middle of 1962 the threat from the inter-continental ballistic missile will undoubtedly be greatly enhanced in numbers, size and accuracy, and the ICBM threat may be supplemented by submarine-launched missiles. By the middle sixties the missile seems likely to be the major threat and the long range bomber relegated to supplementing the major attack by these missiles. It would be only in this period, namely after mid-1962, that the CF-105 could be fully operational in the Royal Canadian Air Force.

"The United States government, after full and sympathetic consideration of proposals that the U.S. Air Force use the *Arrow*, reached the conclusion that it was not economical to do so. Already the U.S. Air Force has decided not to continue with the further development and production of U.S. aircraft having the same general performance as the *Arrow*. The development of interceptor aircraft that is now proceeding in the United States and abroad is on different types.

"Since my announcement of last September much work has been done on the use of a different control system and weapon in the *Arrow*. These changes have been found to be practical.

Although the range of the aircraft has been increased it is still limited. It is estimated that with these changes the total average cost per unit for 100 operational aircraft could be reduced from the figure of about $12,500,000 each to about $7,800,000 each, including weapons, spare parts and the completion of development, but not including any of the sum of $303 million spent on development prior to September last. "The government has taken no decision to acquire other aircraft to replace the CF-100, which is still an effective weapon in the defence of North America against the present bomber threat. The Minister of National Defence and the chiefs of staff are now engaged in further studies of the various alternatives for the improvement of our defences.

"Canadian requirements for civilian aircraft are very small by comparison with this huge defence operation, and frankness demands that I advise that at present there is no other work that the government can assign immediately to the companies that have been working on the *Arrow* and its engine. This decision is a vivid example of the fact that a rapidly changing defence picture requires difficult decisions, and the government regrets its inevitable impact upon production, employment and engineering work in the aircraft and related industries.

"As all in this house will appreciate, this decision has been a very difficult one for the government to take, not only because of the immediate disturbance it is bound to cause to those who have been working on the *Arrow* and related items but because it means terminating a project on which Canada had expended a very large amount of money and in which Canadians have demonstrated the high level of their technical work. However much I might hope that the project be continued in the sense of pride of achievement to avoid immediate dislocations which are regrettable, defence requirements constitute the sole justification for defence procurement.

"Having regard to the information and advice we have received, however, there is no other feasible or justifiable course open to us. We must not abdicate our responsibility to assure that the huge sums which it is our duty to ask parliament to provide for defence are being expended in the most effective way to achieve that purpose.

"Now I wish to turn to another aspect of defence. As previously announced the government has decided to introduce the *Bomarc* guided missile and the SAGE electronic control and computing equipment into the Canadian air defence system, and to extend and strengthen the Pinetree radar control system by adding several additional large radar stations and a number of small gap filler radars. Canadians will be glad to know that agreement in principle with the United States defence department has now been reached on the sharing of the costs of this program.

"Under this arrangement Canada will assume financial responsibility for approximately one-third of the cost of these new projects. The Canadian share will cover the cost of construction of bases and unit equipment, while the United States' share of approximately two-thirds of the cost will cover the acquisition of technical equipment . . .

"As for the technical equipment which is to be financed by the United States, both governments recognize the need for Canada to share in the production of this equipment. Within the principles of production sharing the United States government and the Canadian government expect that a reasonable and fair share of this work will in fact be carried out by Canadian industry . . .

"The government's decisions of last autumn to acquire *Bomarc* missiles for air defence and *Lacrosse* missiles for the Canadian army were based on the best expert advice available on the need to strengthen Canada's air defence against the threat to this continent, and on its determination to continue an effective contribution to the NATO shield.

"The full potential of these defensive weapons is achieved only when they are armed with nuclear warheads. The government is, therefore, examining with the United States government questions connected with the acquisition of nuclear warheads for *Bomarc* and other defensive weapons for use by the

Canadian forces in Canada, and the storage of warheads in Canada. Problems connected with the arming of the Canadian brigade in Europe with short range nuclear weapons for NATO's defence tasks are also being studied.

"We are confident that we shall be able to reach formal agreement with the United States on appropriate means to serve the common objective. It will of course be some time before these weapons will be available for use by Canadian forces . . ."

The Opposition's response in the House was momentarily muted by the sudden shock of the Prime Minister's bombshell. Mr. Diefenbaker had delivered his abrupt and stunning announcement on a Friday, some six weeks before the March 31st deadline earlier intimated as the date for decision, hence the Liberals had the weekend to assess the situation, consider their strategy, and select the main lines of their attack.

The response of A. V. Roe and its employees was instantaneous once the official telegrams ordering cessation of work were received. Avro and Orenda laid off, immediately, all employees engaged on the *Arrow* and *Iroquois* production lines. Some 13,800 men, several hundred of them engineers of the highest qualifications, were put on the streets, most of them that very afternoon. The Prime Minister later denounced this as a blatant attempt by A. V. Roe Canada Ltd. to embarrass the government; but, as already noted, the ineptitude of the government in their handling of the crucial contract termination details was the primary cause of their own acute discomfiture. Even government representatives in the factories were so astounded by the announcement — which reached them via the radio before any official communication was in their hands — that several of them telephoned their departmental superiors unbelievingly for confirmation.

On the production lines men hurled their tools on the floor in anger. Some wept. One man was so shocked that he bundled his belongings into his tool kit and walked out with the crowd, unseeing, not realizing until days later that he had stuffed his blueprints in with his tools. He still has them.

(My personal reaction was one of disbelieving shock. I was a staunch Diefenbaker supporter, as was every member of my family. But my background as a wartime RCAF pilot left me incredulous; I could not credit the Prime Minister's being capable of such a deed. Over the weekend I kept waiting, still unconvinced, hoping for follow-up reports that would explain that the statement had somehow been incomplete, or misunderstood. But by the time Monday had rolled round, with no correction, I was reduced to the adult equivalent of the tearful urchin described in the aftermath of the 1919 Black Sox scandal. With his world collapsed in ruins about him the lad dogged the footsteps of his tainted baseball hero, the great "Shoeless" Joe Jackson, pleading despairingly: "Say it isn't so, Shoeless . . . Say it isn't so.")

The labour unions were stung to fury by the savage suddenness of the termination, and were shortly directing at the government statements couched in the most extreme terms. John Diefenbaker had always identified himself with the common people, the working people, and in truth had done much for their betterment. But this decision struck them as betrayal. Hazen Argue, the Member for Assiniboia, was not diffident about relaying their representatives' vitriolic statements in the House. He cited first a telegram from Mr. P. Podger, the business representative of the International Association of Machinists:

> "The unprecedented callous action of the Diefenbaker government in cancelling the *Arrow* with immediate resultant loss of 13,000 plus jobs is tantamount to economic treachery. The forfeiture of Canadian sovereignty to the U.S. in our defence created by the government's decision calls for the immediate defeat of the Diefenbaker government."

Another telegram was sent by Mr. W. Jacobs, President of the Draftsmen Association of Ontario:

> "Request you use every method available to condemn government for callous treatment of engineering and skilled tradesmen and betrayal to American interests. Government must account for failure to provide substitute work for cancelled *Arrow* project. Demand should be made on Washing-

ton for equitable share defence production. Failing agreement bases should only be established on our terms. If possible force government to go to people to prevent complete take-over by U.S."

Mr. Crawford Gordon, President of A. V. Roe of Canada Ltd., was quoted in the Toronto Globe and Mail:

"As I indicated in my brief statement on Friday, the Prime Minister's announcement cancelling forthwith the *Arrow* and *Iroquois* programs came as a complete surprise to the Company. We received no advance notice whatever of the Friday announcement itself nor did any government department seek prior consultation with the Company to arrange for an orderly and gradual cease-work procedure."

It is worth noting in passing that the balloting in Ontario in subsequent federal elections clearly reflected the Prime Minister's alienation of the skilled labour force in the Toronto-Hamilton heartland, usually a source of solid Tory strength as predictably loyal as the Quebec French-Canadians were to the Liberals. Even if the decision to cancel had been accepted as necessary or justifiable in the national interest, the consequent loss of voting support would have been found unpalatable enough. To the more thoughtful Conservatives across the country, who totally rejected the alleged correctness of the decision, this unnecessary political hemorrhage was doubly galling.

On Monday afternoon, February 23rd, the House of Commons convened at 2:30 p.m. At the earliest opportunity the Hon. Paul Hellyer, the Member for Trinity, a Toronto riding, rose to ask leave to move the adjournment of the House . . . "Under Standing Order 26 for the purpose of discussing a definite matter of urgent public importance, namely the crisis in the aircraft industry involving mass lay-offs and threatened disintegration of this important sector of our Canadian defence production."

In the ensuing debate Mr. Hellyer scored effectively, despite the fact that he was operating under a distinct handicap. His own party, at an earlier stage, had been far from unanimous on the question of proceeding with the development of the *Arrow*, and the

Conservatives were fully aware of the lack of unanimity in Liberal ranks. (General Foulkes, Chairman of the Chiefs of Staff Committee, subsequently made the statement that the Liberals themselves had been on the verge of cancelling the *Arrow* when the 1957 election came along and passed responsibility for the program to their opponents.)

But with a weekend to prepare, and a speech as vulnerable as Mr. Diefenbaker's to dissect, Paul Hellyer was not short of ammunition, despite the fact that he knew Lester Pearson's attack was going to be cautiously focused on the *manner* of the termination rather than the justification therefor. Indeed, any informed critic reading the Prime Minister's superficial essay on the strategic situation would have been sorely tempted to plagiarize Thomas Babington Macaulay and open the rebuttal by pointing out that Mr. Diefenbaker's delicately balanced assessment "deserved the praise, whatever the praise might be worth, of being the best assessment ever delivered by any man on the wrong side of the question of which he was profoundly ignorant".

Mr. Hellyer could have been harsher than he was, notwithstanding the Liberals' handicap; but he launched the debate vigorously. He began by making reference to the fact that he was opening the debate precisely on the fiftieth anniversary of powered flight in Canada, lamenting that, instead of being able to speak about a national celebration, he was constrained by circumstances to deal instead with a national tragedy. He warmed to his task. "The Prime Minister commended those who had designed the aircraft and translated the plans into reality, but then he went on to say that they had been overtaken by events; that the bomber threat had diminished, and that alternative means of defence, presumably against the bombers had been developed much earlier than had been expected.

"It is difficult to understand how the threat from manned bombers could have diminished . . . I am sure from the information we have and from the information we can obtain from technical sources, magazines and other places, that the present inventory of Russian bombers is greater today than at any time in history . . .

"If the alternative means of meeting the threat to which the

Prime Minister alluded is the *Bomarc* missile, some of us would have serious reservations about that, and should like the Prime Minister to give us some more information about it. The *Bomarc* has not yet, to common knowledge, been proven, and early models have been less than satisfactory in performance . . . Observers have also stated that the Russians would still have an inventory of between 1,000 and 2,000 bombers capable of coming over the ice cap and presenting a threat to our national survival. We have been told repeatedly that there is a continuing requirement for manned interceptors. The Minister of National Defence himself said so on several occasions; the supreme commanders of NORAD and his deputy have also made statements to the effect that defence was needed against the manned bomber. They have gone even further and said the *Arrow* was required as part of the defence against the manned bomber.

"Obviously, the government does not think so. In such circumstances the logical question is who is right, the experts or the government ? . . .

"The statement went on to say that the CF-100 was still an effective weapon in the defence of North America against the bomber threat. The Prime Minister's statement should have been more precise. Is the CF-100 still effective against the total Russian capability as far as manned bombers are concerned? Surely the Right Honourable Gentleman is not suggesting that? It is true it might be effective against part of the Russian inventory of bombers, but certainly it would not be effective against their recent jets. As a matter of fact the Air Force placed a requirement for a new version of the CF-100, to be known as the Mark VI, which was to have an afterburner to increase its power and be equipped with an air-to-air guided missile. This was to be a stopgap between the present CF-100, now in squadron service, and the CF-105, but one of the first things the government did when it came to office one and a half years ago was to cancel this requirement.

"The inconsistency of the Prime Minister's statement seemed to lie in the fact that he found it necessary to rationalize the government's decision by speaking of the very extensive cost of the

Arrow. The figures he used were not figures which were common knowledge; they looked as if they had been picked from a hat."

Mr. Hellyer went on to deplore the lack of consideration and consultation on the part of the government in its abrupt cancellation order. He foretold the rapid wasting away of Canada's military aircraft industry and rapidly maturing electronics industry, citing these impending developments as the true cost Canada would pay for buying defence "on the cheap" through the deployment of American *Bomarc* missiles on sites in Canada to be prepared, as their only contribution, by the Canadian government.

"The government has talked much about secondary industry. We well remember the speeches that were made about Canadian development and about the necessity of building up our secondary manufacturing. We do not want to be hewers of wood and drawers of water; we do not want to dig holes for *Bomarc* squadrons; we do not want to be relegated just to cutting down trees and bulldozing boulders out of the way."

The Prime Minister interrupted to ask Mr. Hellyer what explanation he had for the fact that the United States had recently cancelled their F-106C and the F-106D, "of similar capabilities to the CF-105".

Mr. Hellyer knew enough about the subject to lay that argument to rest in five short sentences. "As far as the other planes are concerned, I think we should stop comparing the United States F-106 with our CF-105. They are as different as a horse and buggy and a car. They were not designed to do the same job at all. They were for different military requirements. Perhaps one good reason why the United States should have cancelled their F-105 and F-106 is that they would have looked so poor beside the CF-105."

Angrily Mr. Hellyer went on, pointing out that it was the loss of 20 years of accumulated productive capacity and potential which was so serious. Since the views expressed in a then current Toronto Globe and Mail editorial reflected his own, he read these sentences from it into the record:

"And here is the irony of it. Most Canadians will recall that in the early post-war years we were not permitted to share defence production with the United States; the reason the United States gave being that we lacked the necessary know-how. So at great trouble and cost, we acquired the know-how. Still, there was no sharing. And now, what? Now, the brilliant array of engineering and technical talent which built up this great Canadian industry will be dissipated. Now, these highly-trained men and women — the one national asset — will probably go. Where? To the United States."

After Mr. Hellyer had concluded, Mr. Pearkes rose and gave a full and cogent resumé of the whole *Arrow* program, recounting again the government's failure to get any orders from the United States or Britain for the *Arrow*. Significantly, he indicated, in response to a question from Mr. Hellyer, that if a reasonable order could have been obtained from the United States or the United Kingdom "the government would certainly have given most serious consideration" to going ahead with the *Arrow*. He also confirmed that after being allowed to abandon the development of the Astra Weapons System, the company had given a flyaway cost which he quoted as $3.75 million per copy for the *Arrow*, without spares or missiles.

There was only a minor discrepancy between this figure and the one given by Crawford Gordon the previous autumn. Gordon had publicly committed the company to an estimate that "flyaway cost per aircraft, complete in every respect, including *Iroquois* engines and fire control system, would be $3.5 million for the first hundred and $2.6 million for the next hundred. These costs do not include spares or ground-handling equipment or development and tooling costs."

In the course of his speech Mr. Pearkes made reference to the fact that initially the government had developed some concern over what he implied was the limited range of the *Arrow*. At various times the Prime Minister too spoke critically of the range of the *Arrow*. Unfortunately both these gentlemen tended to mix *radius of action* figures with range figures, the former, of course, being only one-half the true range figure. Futhermore, neither speaker was specific about the assumptions he was making as to the proportion of the flying time during which the aircraft would be on full afterburner power. Most laymen do not appreciate what a complicated question range can be. When a jet fighter goes to full afterburner power the increase in fuel consumption is tremendous. An example or two will suffice to make the point abundantly clear.

Canada is currently considering purchasing a new fighter aircraft. Two of the contenders are the F-16, built by General Dynamics, and the F-14 *Tomcat,* built by Grumman. The manufacturer of the F-16 shows its maximum capability as being over 300 nautical miles with "1.7 hour loiter capability or seven *minutes* combat". The vast difference between seven minutes and one hour and 42 minutes illustrates how radically fuel consumption changes under maximum afterburner conditions — and how precise one has to be, when talking about range, to specify the exact performance to be required during any flight.

In describing the capabilities of the F-14, its manufacturer is careful to avoid generalities. Grumman says that the F-14, with internal fuel only (16,200 pounds), can take off, climb to cruise altitude, fly 500 miles, descend to 10,000 feet, fight in maximum afterburner for two minutes, climb back to cruise altitude, return to base (or carrier), loiter for 20 minutes, and land with five per cent fuel reserve. With that sort of description, airmen have a clear picture of an aircraft's endurance.

As was to be expected of George Pearkes, he was fair in his presentation. He wound up this portion of his speech admitting that, with the additional fuel tanks the company had advised it could instal (once the ASTRA system had been replaced by the Hughes) the *Arrow* would have "a subsonic range of 506 nautical miles". From the context it is safe to state that Mr. Pearkes meant to say a radius of action of 506 nautical miles, i.e., a range of over 1,000 miles.

In a broadcast he made years after the event the Prime Minister referred to the *Arrow* at one point as an aircraft whose endurance, at maximum speed, was only about 20 minutes. Maximum speed means maximum afterburner. Mr. Diefenbaker might have been surprised to learn that the American *Voodoos,* which his government acquired together with the *Starfighters*, in 1961 and 1962, were comparably heavy on fuel. A *Voodoo* pilot whom I spoke to told me that a *Voodoo* at maximum afterburner would use about half its fuel in ten minutes or thereabouts.

The fact is that the *Arrow's* range was not really a factor of any consequence in the final decision[1].

Mr. Pearkes, in his main speech, on February 23rd, 1959, made it clear in three or four different places that budget considerations were extremely important in the decision to cancel the *Arrow*. He laid much more emphasis upon this fact than the Prime Minister had, stating at one point: "If we met all requirements we would be running into a budget far, far higher than the budget for which we are now providing. If we had not taken this action, if we had continued with the CF-105 we would be faced with making a complete change in our defence structure. It might have meant that we would have had to stop the building of such ships as the *Restigouche* and others of that type. That would throw many hundreds of men out of work from our shipyards. We might have had to cut down the strength of the Army or something of that sort. You have to strike a balance."

At a later point in his speech, verifying that the original figure discussed had been 600 *Arrows*, Mr. Pearkes said: "I have checked these figures very carefully. I merely mention that to give an indication of the enormous expense involved and what an utter impossibility it would be for Canada to provide for all the defence of this country."

In a letter he wrote to me in December, 1977, Mr. Pearkes made no reference to obsolescence of the *Arrow*. He said: "The decision to cancel this aircraft was most difficult for all concerned. There just was not enough money to meet all the needs of National Defence. The Navy, and the Army had to be maintained to meet international commitments as well as the Air Force . . . I paid several

1. The commonplace nature of in-flight refuelling should be borne in mind. In September, 1955, the American Navy made in-flight refuelling capability mandatory on all its aircraft. Currently, the F-4 *Phantoms* and F-15 *Eagles* of the USAF's Tactical Air Command routinely fly nonstop from bases in Germany to bases in America, with the *Phantoms* sometimes refuelling as many as eight times in the process.

visits to the United States Department of Defence to see if they would purchase some of the *Arrows,* but they were building new aircraft of their own, their air industry needed all the help their government could give it. I got nowhere. Unless Canada could sell the *Arrow,* the cost would have been prohibitive. The Navy had nothing but older ships, the Army had commitments all over the world. Unless the Government was prepared to assign considerably more money to National Defence, or the needs of the Navy and the Army could be forgotten for a couple of years, there was no money available . . . And so the *Arrow* had to go. The Defence budget was not large enough to meet the demands of all Services and the country had to meet all the postwar demands."

It is fair to say that the *Arrow* died on the altar of economics. Its planned performance was never questioned by any person who was knowledgeable enough to pass judgement.

The debate dragged on, intermittently, for months. Much of the time it was not focused sharply on the central issue of the strategic soundness of the decision, partly because the governments' broad-brush presentation had swept in the related topics of economics, alternative forms of defence, and nebulous future plans for sharing defence work and joining in with the United States on common production ventures. (Regarding the latter, Mr. Hellyer described this as a process that would much resemble Jonah's "joining" the whale.)

Most of the time Mr. Pearson and his cohorts attacked in a distinctly gingerly fashion. They were aware that their own administration had cancelled the *Velvet Glove* missile program, flushing $24,000,000 down the drain, and they were also aware that in 1956 and 1957 a sizeable number of their own supporters had been restless about the increasing costs of the whole *Arrow* program[1]. If the Liberals had been able to enter the fray with clean hands themselves they would undoubtedly have performed with fewer inhibitions and scored more effectively. Even so, they were not short

---

1. At the outset of the Korean war the Liberal government, through Mr. C. D. Howe, had unaccountably "persuaded" Avro to abandon its successfully completed passenger jet, the *Avro Jetliner,* and confine itself to military production.

of ammunition, and the Conservative government seemed incapable of turning around without providing more.

There had been suggestions made by the Opposition — and by Avro as well, so the rumour ran — that the company be allowed to complete *Arrow* No. 6 and fly it, to demonstrate before the world the performance it was capable of with its incomparable *Iroquois* engines. One gathers this was the last thing the government wanted. If the *Iroquois Arrow* performed in accordance with its builders' projections — and its five predecessors had met or exceeded all test demands — its marked superiority to anything then flying would have made the government's considerable embarrassment unbearable.

Thus, after the debate had been in progress only a few weeks, the government made efforts to transfer the *Arrows* to the Royal Aeronautical Establishment in England for the purposes of flying research. The government's effort in this connection was not exposed to public measurement, for they refused to reveal the terms on which they had been prepared to transfer the aircraft to Farnborough; but whatever the scale of effort, it was unsuccessful. In an incredibly stupid and vandalistic move, the government thereupon despatched workmen to Malton with acetylene torches and put the possibility of future constructive suggestions regarding the *Arrows* beyond reach. Under express instructions the workmen torched into ugly and smoking debris ten sleek white machines that represented the most sophisticated objects of the aircraft designer's art in the western world. Apparently the thought of handing the finished aircraft over to the RCAF was never seriously considered. The fact that such a disposition had been the sole object of all effort to date was somehow lost sight of. The *Arrows* were cut to junk.

Challenged to explain this incredible waste, and the barring of all photographers from the scene at the plant, the government tried to assure the House that it really had no alternative, that this was the course any government would have been forced to follow by the rigid demands of national security. The Minister of Defence Production, Mr. O'Hurley, pointed out that under the terms of the agreement with the Americans, i.e., the contract governing the security on the Hughes Weapons System, the Canadian government was justified in refusing to permit any photographers to witness the "dismantling" of the *Arrows*. Pressed by Mr. Hellyer to explain why secrecy was necessary after removal of the weapons systems, Mr. O'Hurley created the impression that the *Arrow* was so sophisticated that it was adorned with classified systems and accoutrements virtually from nose to tail. This differed markedly from the government's earlier portrait of the *Arrow* as a piece of obsolete junk, and Mr. Hellyer enjoyed himself focusing attention on that contradiction:

Mr. O'Hurley: "This was an aircraft constructed not only by Canadian engineers and the Canadian Air Force but also by the United States. It was classified. It could not have been sold on an open market. I do not see any other solution available to the Minister of National Defence but to turn it to scrap. That is the way the situation was."

Mr. Hellyer: "That does not answer my question. I assume there could not have been very much classified material about the plane, because we were told in this House it was obsolescent and that it would not have been useful at the time it was put into squadron service . . . What parts of the plane were classified?

Mr. O'Hurley: "One would practically have to go over the whole plane — hydraulics, fire control, engine, electronic equipment. With the experience which the Hon. Member has with regard to planes he will certainly know that there are hundreds of parts in that plane which were classified. I am certainly not versed enough to give him a complete list of the classified materials in the CF-105 this afternoon."

Mr. Hellyer: "It must have been a good aircraft if there were hundreds of classified parts in it."

Having lent sufficient emphasis to this preliminary point, Mr. Hellyer was challenging the Minister a moment later to tell the House how many of the *Arrows* had actually had fire control apparatus installed in them, and Mr. O'Hurley was retreating with the qualification that if the weapons system was not actually installed "it was definitely there in the plant with other classified material when the cancellation started". Crowded further, he admitted that there was no fire control apparatus installed on Aircraft No. 6 and the other aircraft nearing completion behind it on the production line.

People who purport to know have stated flatly that none of the *Arrows* had the fire control system actually installed. The point is not really material, for even if they had, there would have been no reason in the world why, once it had been removed, the ten aircraft could not have been flown by the RCAF when they had been completed. That point became crystal clear once the government admitted it had made overtures to the Royal Aeronautical Establishment at Farnborough. If security would not have been prejudiced by turning the *Arrows* over to the Royal Aeronautical Establishment, there was clearly no reason why they could not have been turned over to the RCAF for testing and research purposes in Canada. For such a role these aircraft would have been perfectly suited. The plans had called for their being equipped by Avro with a wide range of advanced (and expensive) sensing and recording devices, designed to probe the unexplored frontiers of supersonic flight[1].

It was true that, following Mr. Diefenbaker's speech of September 23rd, 1958, with its urgent directive that costs be pared to the bone, the purchase of much of the sensing and other research equipment had been deferred, hence this expenditure would first have had to be made. But in terms of what had already been spent in bringing the project to the very brink of its full production phase, this incremental cost would have been relatively insignificant — doubly so when measured against the important scientific service these aircraft could have performed.

With those *Arrows* the RCAF could have carried out a comprehensive program of supersonic flight research with planes that would have ensured the cumulative results of their research

---

1. Two of the eleven Concordes flying in the early months of 1979, aircraft which cruise supersonically at 1,320 miles per hour, were not being flown commercially but were used for research and development — not a surprising utilization of these sophisticated aircraft considering that their development cost has been estimated at $2.5 billion.

giving the RCAF and Canada's NATO partners the information base to support technology even more advanced. It is true that only the more experienced pilots could have been permitted to fly these aircraft, at least until the organization of an appropriate training program; but such a restriction would apply in the case of most high performance test aircraft[1]. One RCAF pilot had already flown the *Arrow:* Flight Lieutenant Jack Woodman, from Saskatoon, had been brought in at an early stage to participate in the test flying program with Jan Zurakowski and "Spud" Potocki, the latter Zurakowski's intended successor as chief test pilot. Woodman flew the *Arrow* six times[2].

Apart from the facility it would have provided for testing airframe and weapons system development, the *Arrows* would have provided the ideal test bed on which the RCAF could have launched further development of the *Iroquois* engine, enabling engineers to supplement by air testing the new high altitude test facilities built by Orenda Engines Ltd. There was no doubt whatever that the *Iroquois* was a winner which warranted much further development and exploitation. Mr. Roy T. E. Hurley, the Chairman and President of Curtiss-Wright, had underlined that fact in 1957 when he signed the contact permitting Curtiss-Wright to manufacture and sell the engine under licence in the United States. But all this technological potential, available for modest expenditure, the government discarded with the aeroplanes it burned.

Not a trace of the *Arrow* was to be left. Like mindless Luddites the government ordered every vestige erased, put to the torch — not even one stripped aeroplane was to be allowed to be preserved for posterity in a museum.

The workmen arrived at Malton under peremptory orders, and

---

1. In a letter published in May, 1978, Jan Zurakowski said, contradicting the allegation that only a very skilled pilot could land the *Arrow* without cracking up, "The *Arrow* was not a difficult aircraft to land. Five development *Arrow* aircraft were flown by F/L Jack Woodman, "Spud" Potocki, Peter Cope and myself. Two accidents, which occurred during landing runs (I was involved in one of these), were not related to handling difficulties at all."

2. Jack Woodman is now Director of Flying Operations for Lockheed Aircraft in California. Speaking at a symposium in Winnipeg on May 16th, 1978, he remarked that the *Arrow,* in 1959, had been 20 years ahead of its time.

in an atmosphere appropriate to an execution squad set about their grisly work. They were in the process of lighting their torches when an Avro supervisor warned them that if they did not take proper precautions they might easily injure or kill themselves. He pointed out that many portions of the aircraft were heavily Teflon coated, and that Teflon, when exposed to temperatures of 750° F and upwards, gives off highly toxic fumes of fluorides. Certainly under the nozzle temperatures of 4000° F to 4500° F common with acetylene torches, lethal results could ensue. But for his warning a macabre postscript to the demise of the *Arrow* might have been written.

As it was, the work was continued, outdoors on the hangar apron. The government's determination that this sorry spectacle not be captured on film is easy to understand. Attila the Hun would have sickened and turned away. But while it was relatively easy to keep photographers from walking up to the work site at the plant, the government was unable to hide the scene completely. An enterprising photographer flew over the site despite all their strictures and took aerial photographs of the *Arrows* being nibbled to death, plate-sized pieces of blackened metal lying about their ruined forms like fallen carrion. Not a proud moment in Canada's history.

Within the plant itself some village Hampden had determined, despite the strenuous efforts of the government and the heavy potential sanctions involved, that something was going to be preserved come hell or high water. So, somehow, a complete *Arrow* nose section was surreptitiously moved off the floor and concealed. Its existence was known to only a few people for years, but now it sits in the Canadian National Museum of Science and Technology in Ottawa, a pathetic reminder of an ignoble deed.

While the hapless Mr. O'Hurley was attempting to justify the atrocity in the name of national security, someone should have asked him to compare his government's concept of security requirements with those of our American ally. Three years earlier, in 1956, when the American government cancelled further development of the North-American F-107 in favour of the competing Republic F-105 *Thunderchief*, it first assigned all three F-107's to useful test work, then later took steps to ensure the aircraft's preservation. As a result, the second F-107 is still on display at the Air Force Museum in Ohio. Like the *Arrow*, the F-107 was a highly supersonic and sophisticated aircraft. More to the point, a complete integrated fire control system, the classified XMA-12, had been installed in that second aircraft. The American government apparently experienced no difficulty in maintaining security, and the F-107 sits intact as continuing evidence of their designers' response to the current challenges of aerodynamic progress. Canadians have only the clandestinely preserved truncated nose-section of a far superior aircraft to remind them of their countrymen's technical capabilities.

Chapter 10

Analysis of Prime Minister Diefenbaker's cancellation decision, as explained in his speech of February 20th, 1959, and in subsequent speeches, reveals that decision to have been a major policy error. In terms of magnitude it must rank among the most serious mistakes made by a Canadian politician in peacetime, and it was based upon a culpably restricted assessment of some of the most important factors in the situation.

Mr. Diefenbaker hinged his whole case on the alleged obsolescence of the *Arrow*. The program had been "overtaken by events" to use his euphemistic phraseology. He proposed, therefore, to discard the *Arrow* and to rely upon *Bomarc* missiles backed up by the much older CF-100 aircraft. The *Bomarcs* were to be installed in two Canadian launch sites: one at North Bay, Ontario, the other at La Macaza, Quebec. The *Bomarc* weaponry was to be supplied by the United States on the very favourable terms earlier mentioned. The Americans were extremely anxious to maintain the uniformity of their cross-country line of *Bomarc* installations. The sharp southern dip of the Canada-U.S. boundary through the Great Lakes area posed a strategic problem which this new arrangement would resolve. Some politicians even argued that if, during the negotiations, Canada had pressed to extract the maximum advantage, the American government would have been prepared to provide and staff the installations at North Bay and La Macaza without Canada's even incurring the costs of preparing the sites. But most people felt that the results of the negotiations with our senior NATO partner were reasonable, and that the Prime Minister could not fairly be faulted on that account.

Mr. Diefenbaker's main error lay in a failure to appreciate fully the strict limitations of the *Bomarc*. Coupled with this was a complementary failure to realize that the Russian bomber threat was neither going to remain static nor oblige us by fading away, and that it could not long be dealt with by aircraft like the aging CF-100s. On this latter point his Minister of Defence, George Pearkes, told the House quite candidly on February 23rd that if CF-100s had to tackle Russian bombers of the types known as the *Bear* and the *Bison*, the results would be "touch and go". One was left to imagine what the situation would be if the Russians continued their aircraft development and we did not.

Reference must also be made to the fact that actual results secured in tests of the *Bomarcs* had been far from satisfactory. In 1959 the first models were still quite unreliable against high speed targets, although the new models that Canada was to receive showed promise of being considerably better. But the bald fact, which the Prime Minister never seemed to grasp, is that even a fully reliable surface-to-air missile and a manned interceptor are not interchangeable weapons.

Both can attack an intruding aircraft. The problem is that most "intruding" aircraft turn out to be friendly, and a missile, once it has been launched from the ground toward its target, cannot tell the difference and turn harmlessly away at the last minute. The recurring situation is that unidentified aircraft almost always prove on investigation to be friendly civilian or commercial aircraft whose pilots have simply failed to file flight plans, or have wandered far off their intended track. The most recent example highlights the problem, but it has been one of long standing.

In April, 1978, a Korean Airlines Boeing 707, loaded with passengers, unaccountably suffered a malfunction of its navigational systems, causing the pilot to veer far off his course, and, eventually to violate the airspace of the Soviet Union in a threatening manner in a most sensitive area. The passenger aircraft was intercepted by Soviet fighters, and finally fired upon and forced to land. If the Russians had simply launched a surface-to-air missile at the aeroplane and destroyed the 200 or so people aboard, the rest of the world would have been outraged, and international tensions would undoubtedly have increased.

At the time of the *Arrow* cancellation it was not uncommon to have Canadian fighter pilots scrambling several times a day to fly out and visually check unidentified aircraft picked up on radar. This function could not be delegated to missiles. Neither could it safely be left to obsolescent aircraft — which the CF-100 was at that time — that were hard put to make the necessary interceptions against speedy targets, and which could be eluded with relative ease by aircraft whose performance represented only a slight improvement over the enemy's existing inventory.

Even where targets can safely be taken to be hostile, interception by manned aircraft rather than by a ballistic missile has always imported substantial advantages for the defender attempting to carry out the interception. Firstly, the aircraft normally carries six or eight missiles, not the single warhead of a surface-to-air missile. The crew of the manned interceptor can take steps, should these prove necessary, to neutralize the electronic countermeasures of the target, something no missile is yet capable of doing. Furthermore, the manned interceptor can engage a group of hostile targets in a logical priority. For example, a damaged attacker that had jettisoned its bombs and was turning to flee would automatically be accorded a much lower priority than the nearest inbound undamaged attacker. Similarly, decoys launched by the various target aircraft could be filtered out and ignored by the crew of the manned interceptor and their attack brought to bear upon the real targets.

All these basic points were known in every camp; indeed they were so obvious that airmen everywhere watched the debate in the Canadian House of Commons with a certain degree of incredulity. After all, the *Bomarc* was certainly not an anti-missile missile; that weapon was not in anyone's armory. And yet Mr. Diefenbaker somehow seemed to be implying that by building two *Bomarc* sites, whose weapons would have a "one-way range" of approximately 400 miles[1], Canadians were modernizing their defence to match the growing ICBM threat of the Russians.

Moving to *Bomarcs* as the third element of the basic three element defence concept was entirely sound — those three elements being SAGE (the radar detection and computer capability of the "Semi-Automatic Ground Environment"), manned interceptors, and surface-to-air missiles.

But down-grading or scrapping the most important element of the three was irrational.

Mr. Diefenbaker had assured the country on February 20th that he was acting on the best information and advice. His government, he said, had "made a thorough examination in the light of all the information available . . ." He went on to assert: "Having regard to the information and advice we have received, however, there is no other feasible or justifiable course open to us." Three days later, after alluding to a newspaper reporter's statement that Mr. C. D. Howe ". . . admitted yesterday (February 20th) that rapid development of electronics and guided missiles overtook the *Arrow* . . ." Mr. Diefenbaker harked back to the advice and information underlying his decision saying:

"Why was it stopped? Well, sir, it was stopped for the reason that the Chiefs of Staff, who advise in their wisdom and on the

---

1. The actual range of the *Bomarc* units at North Bay and La Macaza was only 130 miles, not 400 miles. As Charles Grinyer explains: "It was generally accepted that the ultimate range with this weapon was 400 miles, but this required a new propulsion system which was never developed. About mid-1958 Orenda was asked to look into an engine which used a special fuel 'Isopropylacetylene'. This had the combined property of changing into a vapour like steam when heated and could be burned like gasoline or jet fuel. This permitted a type of steam turbine with an afterburner. With such an engine, the *Bomarc* was able to discard the solid rockets and the ram-jets. However, although we could design the engine within the weight limitations, the fuel was another matter altogether, as it was very unstable and dangerous. I have forgotten my estimate to develop this concept but it was nearly as high as for the *Iroquois*."

Above: *Prime Minister, the Right Honourable John G. Diefenbaker. An able and dedicated parliamentarian, he won the greatest electoral victory in Canada's history; but he never developed any real feel for Canada's special role as a western air power; neither did he grasp the full ramifications of his action in destroying Canada's facilities for military aircraft design and testing.* (PAC)

Below left: *Honourable George Pearkes, V.C., Minister of National Defence in the Diefenbaker government.*

Below right: *Prime Minister Lester B. Pearson. His reversal of policy on the issue of installing nuclear warheads on Canada's Bomarcs helped him to defeat the Diefenbaker administration in 1963.*

137

Above: *Paul Hellyer, Defence critic for the Liberal Party in 1958. Hellyer was an effective critic during the debate on the Arrow cancellation; but in 1966, as Minister of Defence himself, he was the prime sponsor of the "Unification" Bill which many people regarded as the most damaging blow ever inflicted upon Canada's armed forces by any administration.*

Above: *General Charles Foulkes. Chairman of the Canadian Chiefs of Staff. Foulkes tried to obtain a unanimous recommendation from the Chiefs to cancel the Arrow; but the Chief of Air Staff, Air Marshal Hugh Campbell, adamantly refused to recommend that short-sighted policy.*

Right: *Air Marshal Hugh Campbell, Chief of Air Staff, RCAF, 1957-1962. Air Marshal Campbell, and his Deputy, Air Marshal C. R. Dunlap, were both convinced of the necessity of retaining manned interceptor aircraft as an element in a balanced defence force. Air Marshal Campbell fought against cancellation of the Arrow to the bitter end.*
(PAC PL-110200)

138

Above: *A CF-100 Mk5, 18551, of 410 Sqn. Uplands, seen in formation with a Convair F-102 Delta Dagger of the USAF's Air Defence Command during a NORAD exercise over Newfoundland in 1958. The F-102 prototype first flew in October 1953 but required extensive redesign to overcome serious aerodynamic problems.*

Below: *A considerable amount of effort had to be expended to refine the F-102 design to produce an interceptor with satisfactory capability. The end product was the F-106 Delta Dart, first flown in December, 1956. With its single-seat, single-engine configuration it was not considered suitable for Canadian requirements.*

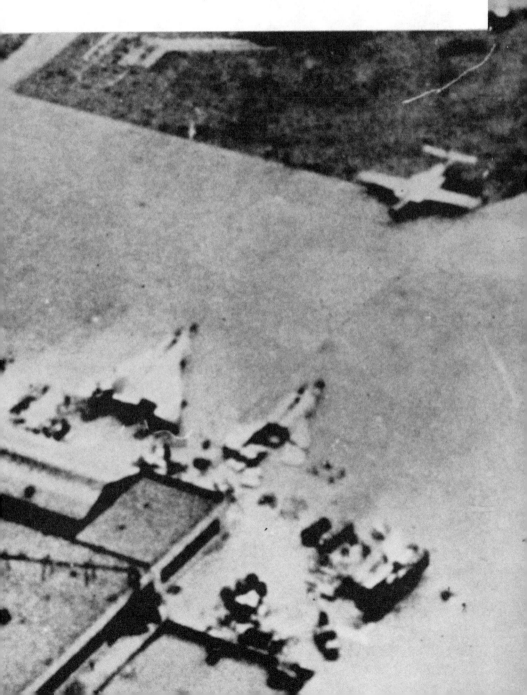

The Diefenbaker government ordered all photographers excluded from the area while this $125,000,000 act of vandalism was perpetrated. They succeeded in keeping photographers on the ground away from the area; but one photographer took to the air to obtain this shot of the Arrow being hacked to death on the tarmac in front of the Avro Aircraft hangars. The stricken Arrow on the right lies collapsed, with the bulk of the right mainplane hacked off. This picture is perhaps the best commentary on the whole sorry affair.

(AIR AND SPACE DIVISION, NATIONAL MUSEUM, OTTAWA)

Above: *A recent photograph of Air Marshal (retired) Hugh Campbell, published following his elevation to the chairmanship of the Board of Directors of Phillips Cables Ltd. in May, 1978.* (PHILLIPS CABLES LTD.)

Below: *General Thomas D. White, Chief of Staff, U.S. Air Force. This photo taken January 4th, 1960.*
(USAF)

Above: *Air Marshal C. R. Slemon, appointed in 1957 as the first Deputy Commander of NORAD.*

Below: *General Nathan F. Twining, of the U.S. Air Force, photographed May 9th, 1958.* (USAF)

142

Above: *General Earle E. Partridge, Commanding Officer Air Defence Command, photographed October 16th, 1955. In 1957 General Partridge became the first Commander of NORAD, and shared the views regarding the necessity for manned interceptors expressed by Air Marshal Slemon in November, 1958.*
(USAF)

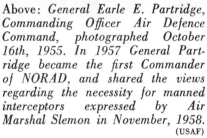

Above right: *General Curtis LeMay. Photograph taken August 28th, 1962. General LeMay was fully cognizant of the limitations attaching to missiles, and of the need for balanced forces.* (USAF)

Right Centre: *Honourable Neil H. McElroy, photographed January 20th, 1958. Mr. McElroy was Secretary of the Air Force, and initially his department was most sympathetic and helpful regarding the development of the Arrow. An American order, even of limited dimensions, would probably have kept the Arrow alive; but there were factors at work militating against that decision.*
(USAF)

Right: *Air Marshal C. R. Dunlap, Deputy Chief of Air Staff, 1959. Like Air Marshal Campbell he opposed cancellation of the Arrow.*
(RCAF)

143

Above: *An American Bomarc missile at rest in its bin.* (BOEING)

Below left: *A Bomarc erected and ready to launch.* (BOEING)

Below right: *A Bomarc at moment of launch.* (CAF)

basis of the best information they can secure, determined that it did not make sense to expend the amount in question on behalf of this phase of defence, having regard to the development of missiles and the like in the last few years."

A few moments later he underlined his original thesis:

"I realize that defence production is an important weapon in the battle against unemployment. However, I say with all the seriousness that I can put at my command, that the production of obsolete weapons as a make-work program is an unjustifiable expenditure of public funds."

The Prime Minister went on to underline, unwittingly, his profound lack of understanding of the differing roles and capabilities of manned interceptors and surface-to-air missiles:

"The minister placed on the record today a general indication of the area which would be protected against attacks at supersonic speeds. On the other hand, we have available to us the *Bomarc*, whose area of defence and defensive action is not far removed from that of the CF-105, but the difference in expenditure has been clearly set out. The cost of the *Bomarc* missile to Canada, as compared to the $781 million of the CF-105, is approximately $110.8 million. That represents something that must be taken into consideration, all things being equal *and the defensive properties of each being about the same.*" [author's italics.]

Examine firstly Mr. Diefenbaker's statement that his decision was founded on a conclusion reached by the Chiefs of Staff. That statement was technically correct, and Mr. Diefenbaker had the documentation to prove it. But he was being less than candid under the circumstances in failing to reveal that one Chief of Staff, Air Marshal Hugh Campbell, his Chief of Air Staff, was strenuously opposed to the cancellation of the *Arrow* and at no time ever concurred with that proposal. Had the Chiefs of Staff Committee been unanimous in the recommendation, protocol ordained that the recommendation be so attributed, i.e., to the Chiefs of Staff *Committee.* Since in this case there had not been unanimity of the voting members, the Chairman, General Foulkes, simply attributed it to the "Chiefs of Staff". The inflexibly dissenting view of the Chief of Air Staff was not publicized by the Prime Minister.

It goes without saying that the Prime Minister was entitled to overrule his Chief of Air Staff on this question. Indeed, his government was entitled to overrule a unanimous Chiefs of Staff Committee recommendation, although the political repercussions of such a step might well be terminal in most situations. But to overrule his Chief of Air Staff on a matter like this was a surprising step for Mr. Diefenbaker to take.

To reject his air expert's professional advice on a question that really turned on the effectiveness of an aeroplane, and to accept instead the advice of Navy experts and Army generals, was indefensible — if indeed the case hinged, as Mr. Diefenbaker said it did, on the obsolescence of the aeroplane. The parallel, in everyday life, would be to reject the considered advice of a respected legal counsel and ask one's medical advisor instead to pass judgment on the legal points involved in a proposed building contract — or to seek a dentist's or architect's reassurance on the appropriate drafting of one's will.

The evaluation of the relative effectiveness of the basic elements of the air defence structure was clearly a question in connection with which the other Chiefs would rely substantially upon the Chief of Air Staff for guidance. Any admiral or general would shrink from overruling the air specialist on a vitally important technical point involving the airman's field, just as the Chief of Air Staff would obviously defer to the generals on the rating to be given competing tanks or guns, or to the admirals on a question of naval ordnance. One is therefore forced to conclude that in this case the question put to the Chiefs of Staff was not simply to pass judgment on the strategic and tactical value of the interceptor; the reasonable inference is that the other Chiefs felt constrained to adopt the stance they did by the economic limitations imposed upon them by the government, and to rebel against further reductions or continuing deferrals in their own fields of responsibility. There is no doubt that in the eyes of the other Chiefs the completion of the *Arrow* program meant a continuing disproportionate share of the Defence budget going to the RCAF.

But the Prime Minister was not laboring under any misapprehension about the position of the Chief of Air Staff. If Mr. Diefenbaker was going to justify the cancellation of the *Arrow* on strategic grounds, i.e., on its alleged obsolescence, and attribute that opinion by implication to the Chiefs of Staff, surely he owed it to his peers in the House to acknowledge that the professional opinion of his expert air advisor, the Chief of Air Staff, was firmly to the contrary, and that Air Marshal Campbell opposed the cancellation.

On the question of the urgent need for the best manned interceptor available — and no one challenged the *Arrow's* qualifications on that score — Air Marshal Hugh Campbell had overwhelming professional support, and not just in Canadian circles. Before, during, and after this period, eminent airmen in the United States were making the point. Their views were firmly stated, frequently before a United States Senate Subcommittee, and were widely known. They were certainly known in detail to Air Marshal Hugh Campbell, to his deputy, Air Marshal C. R. Dunlap, and to the Deputy Minister of National Defence, former Air Marshal Frank Miller. Through these people, apart altogether from the broad newspaper and magazine coverage given them, the views of the leading American professionals were available for relay to the government. In light of Mr. Diefenbaker's statements, and the later developments, they make interesting reading.

On the question of the indispensability of the manned interceptor, USAF General Earle Partridge, the Commander of NORAD, was in complete accord with his deputy commander, Air Marshal Roy Slemon. It will be recalled that Air Marshal Slemon's statement, which preceded the Prime Minister's cancellation announcement by three months, flatly contradicted Mr. Diefenbaker's thesis. General Partridge had stood with Air Marshal Slemon when he made that statement. General Partridge himself had made the point on more than one occasion that *Bomarcs* simply could not discharge the same function as a manned interceptor. He had explained that *Bomarcs* were designed basically for limited point defence, and that NORAD's obvious task was to intercept attackers as far away as possible. This presupposed first identifying them positively as hostile, and then relaying that information to Command — tasks that simply could not be performed by a missile. Discharging the task, in his opinion, called for NORAD's having the fastest possible long-range interceptor for as far into the future as could be foreseen.

General Curtis E. LeMay, USAF, had stated publicly:

"Our ballistic missiles have not yet demonstrated the type of reliability or accuracy which is required to ensure the most effective use of the relatively small yield warheads which they carry . . .

"Even after missiles achieve the reliability and accuracy they now lack . . . there will always be a requirement for a mixture of manned and unmanned weapon systems."

General Nathan F. Twining, USAF, was reported to have expressed his belief that the Russians were building a new bomber with a performance much superior to that of their *Bear* or *Bison*. These latter aircraft were the ones Mr. Pearkes said would pose a "touch and go" situation if we had only CF-100s to effect their interception, the CF-100 being able to handle with assurance only the much older Russian *Badger*.

General Thomas White, Chief of Staff, USAF, gave testimony before a Subcommittee confirming General Twining's opinions. General White expatiated upon the fact that, to a nation contemplating a nuclear attack, a bomber retained distinct advantages over an ICBM in that the bomber could carry a wide range of nuclear weapons, varying in yield and capability. Thus the bomber clearly had a much greater potential for use in limited war. This information, coupled with General Twining's warning of the new Russian bomber, the *Bounder*, certainly did not square with Mr. Diefenbaker's view of a diminishing Russian bomber threat, and the Prime Minister's homey explanation to the House on March 3rd that:

"There is no purpose in manufacturing horse collars when horses no longer exist."

General Twining had been quoted in the 1958 Annual edition

of Canadian Aviation regarding the most effective composition of an air force:

"In the future . . . I see integrated forces of manned and unmanned systems . . . It will take both manned and unmanned systems to perform our mission, because in the future the essentials for success will still be quick reaction, reliability, flexibility and versatility. If manned systems can perform some tasks better, we want manned systems . . ."

It is not an exaggeration to say that on the central question of the recognition of the vital role required to be discharged by supersonic manned interceptors, virtually the whole U.S. defence establishment, from Secretary of Defence McElroy on down, held views directly opposed to those expressed by Mr. Diefenbaker. Although the U.S. abandoned several interceptor programs in the process, including that of the F-108, it carried on the development of the type vigorously. The record makes it clear that it would have been a difficult assignment to find a senior airman anywhere in Canada or the United States who shared Mr. Diefenbaker's theories concerning the redundancy of manned interceptors. The impression he conveyed in his various speeches after the event, to the effect that he had canvassed the best professional advice and information, has to be judged in the knowledge that his own Chief of Air Staff held views diametrically opposed to his own, as did the Deputy Chief, the Commander of NORAD, the Deputy Commander of NORAD, and the senior American airmen listed. George Pearkes' candid recollection was that Hugh Campbell, the Chief of Air Staff, was brokenhearted over the decision to cancel.

Having killed what was probably the best fighter in the western world in 1959, Mr. Diefenbaker soon had his government negotiating for the acquisition of American-designed fighters, namely, F-101 *Voodoos* and F-104 *Starfighters*. Canada began to receive them in 1961. As of this date, late 1978, we are still using them, along with American-designed Northrop F-5s. The *Voodoos* are scheduled to remain in service in their interceptor role until Canada's new fighter program brings their replacement into squadron service in 1983.

Today, twenty years after Prime Minister Diefenbaker

announced the demise of manned interceptors, and destroyed Canada's capability to design and build her own, Canada is preparing to spend 2.34 billion dollars to buy manned interceptors from either the United States or Britain. The United States is marketing four or five highly advanced interceptors at the moment, including the Grumman F-14 *Tomcat,* the McDonnell Douglas F-15 *Eagle,* General Dynamics' F-16, and two versions of the Northrop-McDonnell F-18. Britain, West Germany and Italy have sponsored production of another fighter that can discharge both the interceptor and the ground interdiction role, the Panavia *Tornado;* and the French firm of Dassault Breguet is in the process of going into production in the latest of its series of *Mirage* interceptors — the new *Mirage 2000.* Until February 1st, 1978, the latter aircraft was another competitor in Canada's new fighter program.

All this activity reflects a strong and growing demand for more and more manned interceptors — to meet a correspondingly enhanced threat from Russian bombers. That threat has grown along the lines anticipated back in 1958 by airmen like General Twining. The U.S. is selling interceptors (F-15 *Eagles*) to Saudi Arabia and to Israel, supplementing the Northrop F-5s it sold in that area some time ago. The consortium backed by the governments of Britain, West Germany and Italy, is building Panavia *Tornados* in large numbers for the air forces of those countries, and is energetically marketing the plane elsewhere.

One ironic sidelight: the Panavia *Tornado* is one of the six aircraft competing for the Canadian government's current contract for 130 - 150 new fighters for interceptor and ground attack duties. The *Tornado* is an excellent aircraft by all accounts, equipped with highly advanced avionics equipment. The ironic item of information is that its maximum speed is reputed to be Mach 2.2. If Canada buys the *Tornado,* we will be buying an aircraft 200 m.p.h. slower than the Mach 2.5 speed projected for the Mark III *Arrow* in 1959. (For public consumption the F-14 *Tomcat* has a quoted maximum design speed of Mach 2.34; the F-15 *Eagle's* is reportedly Mach 2.3; and General Dynamics' F-16A has a reported maximum speed of Mach 2.2.) The Panavia *Tornado* is reported to cost approximately 20 million dollars per copy, close to the 17 million quoted for a Northrop F-18L. The *Tomcat* is said to cost 26 million dollars per copy now. Even taking account of inflation factors, the 3.75 million per aircraft for the *Arrow* in 1959 looks attractive.

Carl Lindow, the former Avro design specialist, now a consultant with Boeing in Seattle, said this of the *Arrow*, in 1977:

"If the *Arrow* had been built, there would not be an aeroplane that could equal it today except the Grumman F-14 with its *Phoenix* missiles."

In 1975, Norway, Denmark, Holland and Belgium entered into a $2.2 billion contract to acquire 348 General Dynamics' F-16 interceptors on a co-operative basis. The arrangements were sanctioned by the U.S. Defence Department, and contemplated European production of 58% of the work — much of it going to Belgium's Fabrique Nationale Herstal, which will build the Pratt & Whitney F100-PW-100 jet engines under licence. Japan recently elected, after testing several interceptors, to purchase McDonnell-Douglas F-15 *Eagles* as its basic air defence weapon. The Russian bomber threat is more acute now than at any time heretofore, and the Soviet Union's *Backfire-B* bomber is of sufficient concern to the United States government that the discontinuance of that aircraft is an item on the agenda of the SALT II talks. The *Backfire-B* has the capability, with the now routine procedure of airborne refuelling, of carrying nuclear bombs at supersonic speeds from Russia to the United States, and then returning to base. The supersonic speeds alluded to have been estimated at various figures up to 1850 m.p.h. (Mach 2.76).

The air threat has not only been maintained, it has been varied and intensified by the Russian practice of operating bombers from bases in Cuba. Those aircraft have frequently probed the radar defences of the U.S., and on at least one occasion they successfully hoodwinked American radar operators by using new electronic countermeasures. The air threat will be further intensified. The Soviet Union has announced the launching of a construction program to build no less than ten aircraft carriers. A sizeable proportion of these will doubtless be deployed in positions threatening a whole range of North American targets. Manned interceptors capable of dealing with their ship-borne fighter-bombers, as well as with long-range bombers, will have to be acquired by NORAD. The mobile Russian bases represented by these aircraft carriers will probably bring close to North American shores, in due course, ship-borne variants of the best Russian fighters and fighter-bombers, including the MIG-25 *Foxbat*, the MIG-27 *Flogger-D*, the SU-19 *Fencer*, and the SU-20 *Fitter-B*. These will be added to the threat of the long-range bombers such as the TU-26 *Backfire*, the TU-95 *Bear-D* and the TU-16 *Badger-C*. The capabilities that our American allies attribute to at least some of these aircraft can be deduced from the fact that F-15 *Eagles* have practised (with considerable success) downing simulated MIG-25 *Foxbats* flying at Mach 2.7 at 70,000 feet. (The F-15, the fastest climbing aircraft in the world, has an official service ceiling of 63,000 feet. The service ceiling projected for the *Arrow* Mark III in 1959 was 60,000 feet.)

The aerial threat has certainly not diminished. Manned interceptors remain vitally important, and will for some time to come.

The fighter aircraft now to be purchased by Canada from foreign suppliers will be built to have a service life of approximately 20 years, so that, barring unforeseen developments, the manned interceptors that Prime Minister Diefenbaker assumed were on their way out in 1959 will be on the job as the year 2000 rolls around.

Speaking in Blackpool in 1977 to the annual conference of the RAF Association, Air Chief Marshal Sir Neil Cameron, at that time Britain's Chief of Air Staff, gave a strong endorsement to the Panavia *Tornado*, and explained again why manned interceptors cannot, even now, be retired:

"If unmanned vehicles could be developed to take on some of the roles of airpower this would be welcomed, but there is no doubt about the future of manned aircraft.

"The human brain weighs [some] forty ounces, but it does have two very important qualities . . . it can relate seemingly unrelated items in decision-making, and it can react to the unforeseen and improvise. Make no mistake, the manned *aircraft stays with us."*

The similarity between that 1977 message and the one beamed at Ottawa in November, 1958, by the Deputy Commander of NORAD ("for as long as we can see we must have manned interceptors . . .") is striking, to say the least.

Reviewing, as objectively as possible, the evidence available to the government in 1958 and 1959, it is tempting to oversimplify and sum up in the words H. L. Mencken applied to the "solution" suggested for an earlier problem and say that the government's decision was "simple, clear, bold and idiotic".

In fairness to the Diefenbaker government, however, one has to underline the fact recorded by General Foulkes, namely, that there was a distinct likelihood that the Liberal government, had it been returned to office in 1957 or 1958, would have followed exactly the same course and cancelled the *Arrow* themselves. A party that could prostitute itself in wartime over the conscription issue, for the sake of electoral support in one province, as the federal Liberals did so blatantly in World War II, was hardly to be counted upon to risk anything for national security in 1959, particularly if the economics began to look troublesome. If more recent evidence was required, their abandonment of the *Velvet Glove* missile development program did not constitute a reassuring endorsement of their proclivities; neither did their termination of the successful Avro *Jetliner*.

Despite the fact that Mr. Diefenbaker hung his case for cancellation on the technical point of obsolescence, the record is replete with evidence that the economics of the program was really the dominant factor, consciously or unconsciously[1]. On this point too the decision seems to have been a most serious error, particularly in view of its long-term effects on Canada's economy. Mr. Diefenbaker's political hero, Sir John A. MacDonald, architect of the federal

---

1. Air Vice-Marshall Easton, who had been the Air Member for Technical Services for over six months at the time of the cancellation, reviewed the "economics" arguments in his correspondence with me, then, referring to the Prime Minister's cancellation speech, stated: "The other arguments used in the cancellation announcements *were not consistent with the advice received* . . ." — referring to the support *for* the *Arrow* emanating from the senior RCAF personnel right up to and including the Chief of Air Staff.

Conservatives' "National Policy", would have repudiated his successor's actions in incredulous outrage.

On Mr. Diefenbaker's own figures, getting 100 *Arrows* into squadron service by 1962 was going to cost the government 780 million dollars. Since Crawford Gordon had given Avro's figures, according to George Pearkes, as 3.75 million dollars per copy, flyaway cost, Mr. Diefenbaker's figure of 780 million for 100 aircraft obviously included a generous allowance for the extraneous items of weapons and spares, plus the cost of completing the technically important development program. But even on Mr. Diefenbaker's own figures, 780 million dollars over the three years until 1962 meant 260 million dollars per year. With Canada preparing to spend roughly ten times that amount in 1979, to purchase 130 - 150 new fighters which will have been designed and tested elsewhere, 260 million dollars seems a reasonable amount for 100 fighters of excellent capabilities.

The figure sounds even more reasonable when one considers that more than half of it would quickly be returned to the government, largely in the form of corporate and personal income taxes. (The Financial Post estimated the figure at 65 per cent late in 1959.) If the "net" figure were thus reduced by half, say to a total of 130 million each year for three years, representing the portion to be picked up by taxpayers other than those receiving the government payout, the value standards adopted by the government are difficult to appreciate. If that aspect of Canada's national security was not worth an annual amount of 130 million dollars, taking into account also the 30,000 jobs the industry was sustaining while turning out the world's best interceptor, our scale of values seems to require re-examination. But take Mr. Diefenbaker's gross figure of 260 million dollars per year and consider these facts:

Sweden is a country with a population and an economy about one-third the size of Canada's. (Its 1974 population figure is shown as 8.3 million, compared with Canada's 22.7 million. Sweden's estimated G.N.P. in 1974 was $56.2 billion, Canada's $150.3 billion.) Yet Sweden, over the years, has maintained its military aircraft industry, and is currently producing both the supersonic

Viggen interceptor (Mach 2+) and the Saab 105G twin jet trainer and light attack aircraft. The latter is in use in the Austrian Air Force and the Royal Swedish Air Force.

Israel, truly a Lilliputian by comparison with Canada, is designing an advanced supersonic interceptor as an alternative to the American F-16 built by General Dynamics. While the government of Israel has not yet given a firm commitment to the builder, Israel Aircraft Industries Ltd., the Defence and Foreign Relations Committee of the Knesset has given a strong recommendation that the project receive the go-ahead from the government. At the outset it was estimated that the development of a prototype would cost $250 million. That estimate has now been revised upwards to $560 million; still the Defence and Foreign Relations Committee has recommended it in a lopsided vote, recognizing the fact that such weapons are too important to the security of the country to be left to the discretion of outside sources.

Perhaps the most thought-provoking fact, however, in trying to assess Canada's perspective, is that while Canada as a nation could not afford 260 million dollars a year for the *Arrow* in 1959, the City of Montreal spent one billion, six hundred million dollars in 1976 to host the Olympic Games. That expenditure for sport and entertainment, taking into account the volume discounts quoted by Avro at the beginning of 1959, would have paid for more than 600 *Arrows*.

Chapter 11

Following World War II, the immigration policy of successive Canadian governments had been progessively tightened in an attempt to limit the entry of new citizens to those having useful and highly developed skills, people equipped to make a positive contribution to Canadian society. With his decision to cancel the *Arrow*, Prime Minister Diefenbaker threw away, in one instant, the results of years of effort by both government and private industry, forcing a mass exodus of highly skilled craftsmen and professionals to the aero-space industry in the United States. Selective immigration and recruitment alone could not have attracted to Canada in 20 years what the *Arrow* cancellation lost the country overnight. It is very doubtful that a cadre of design, testing and fabricating specialists of their calibre will ever be assembled in Canada again.

The vital elements of the military aircraft and engine industry were reduced to a remnant by the blow, at least in respect of top design and testing personnel. Canada preserved half or three-quarters of its capacity to assemble aircraft, but threw away almost entirely its most prized asset in the form of the teams of aero-engineers and designers, the testing specialists, and the weapons system computer and electronic experts.

Between the original designing of a high performance aircraft and its ultimate appearance rolling off a production line, there is a gap of approximately six years. While one new aircraft is going into squadron service, the plans for its successor are already well advanced. By voluntarily giving up the design and testing capability represented by the highly successful Avro and Orenda teams, among the world's leaders at that point, Canada put itself back into the position it had been in many years earlier, the position that Air Marshal Curtis and others with his insight had struggled to overcome. During World War II the infant military aircraft industry in Canada had built and assembled aircraft that had been designed and tested elsewhere years earlier. With the demise of the *Arrow,* after briefly leading the world in the field of military aircraft design, Canada reverted to its former humble role.

Under the current New Fighter Program, Canada will insist on securing industrial offsets on the purchase of 2.34 billion dollars worth of American or British fighters. Part of those industrial offsets will undoubtedly appear in the form of contracts given Canadian firms — or Canadian subsidiaries of American firms — to build under licence the products of foreign design. The chances are it will be an American design. While we are assembling those aircraft, and paying direct or indirect royalties to American firms for the privilege, the designers in those American firms will be working six years ahead of Canadians; their metal fabricators and toolmakers, their fibre optics technicians, and their electronics people, will all be expanding their technology a comparable interval ahead of Canadians', increasing their efficiency in new techniques and consolidating, probably irreversibly, an advantage that a segment of Canadian industry once held over them. Canada threw that away on February 20th, 1959.

The very day of the cancellation announcement A. V. Roe released from the affected subsidiaries almost 14,000 workers. It was estimated that another 15,000 or 16,000 tradesmen, employed by the 2,500 suppliers of Avro and Orenda, also lost their jobs, bringing the total number unemployed as a result of the cancellation to 30,000. Although it was ineptitude on the part of the government that caused this in the first instance, one cannot examine the record without feeling that Crawford Gordon, had he wanted to put forth the effort, could have softened the blow, at least during a brief transitional period[1]. In the absence of some new arrangements being negotiated, the penalties flowing from contract termination were all spelled out in the agreements, and the record suggests that a little goodwill, not to say compassion, on the part of Mr. Gordon, could at least have reduced the savage suddenness of the trauma. Instead, it would appear, he chose to assume the role of the injured innocent, take the inadequately detailed standard termination notices at face value, stand on his strict legal rights, and throw everyone onto the streets as abruptly as possible to occasion the government the maximum possible political embarrassment. A telephone call to the Prime Minister or to Mr. O'Hurley to point up the inadequacy of the official notices would probably have sufficed, given the political leverage the cancellation automatically provided; but in the tension of the strained relationship existing between the Prime Minister and the President of A. V. Roe, nothing was done[2].

People whose skills Canada could ill afford to lose started to leave almost immediately. Most of them left with great reluctance — and with great bitterness toward the government that valued them so cheaply. Fred Matthews sent applications as quickly as he could

---

1. It is interesting to note that, according to one reporter, the termination costs built into the various contracts ran to more than what it would have cost to finish the first 37 *Arrows* on the development contract and wind the whole operation down in an orderly fashion.

2. Two things should, in fairness, be borne in mind: (1) There had been earlier attempts on the part of the company to avoid the need for this sort of abrupt cessation of work; (2) On February 20th there was some contact made by Avro, although not through Crawford Gordon's office, in an effort to warn the government of the impending consequences. Fred Smye, Chief Executive Officer of Avro and Orenda in 1959, wrote a gracious letter to the author pointing out that ". . . we continually pleaded with the government to let us know what was going on. We asked them to inform us if they had or were about to decide to cancel, as we could work out with them the best way to carry it out. These pleas fell on very deaf ears. We advised them what would happen in the event of an abrupt termination. Furthermore the company was technically on the hook and deliberately placed there to the tune of about $50,000,000. It must be remembered that the cancellation statement said that no other work would be available to the company.

"Gordon Hunter called me at 10:00 a.m. to inform the company of the cancellation. We received the telegrams at about 1:00 p.m. I phoned Hunter at 2:00 p.m. to advise him and for him to advise the P.M. of our intended action at 4:00 p.m. As we heard nothing from the government, we had no alternative but to proceed. That was a terrible day."

write them to no less than 40 companies in Canada. He received not so much as a single acknowledgement. A man possessing the technical qualifications to discharge successfully the responsibilities of Supervisor of Experimental Flight Test Engineering on one of the most advanced supersonic aircraft in the world was apparently not needed in Canada. In a few weeks the most highly skilled work force ever assembled here disappeared like spring snow in a chinook.

Craftsmen like E. J. Silling and H. C. Ralph, people with a wealth of experience making them almost invaluable in a plant as innovators and as mentors to younger tradesmen, moved away to join American firms and contribute their skills to another economy. Today each manages his own business in the United States. Carl Lindow, one of the original design team on the CF-100, wound up in Seattle. (Today he runs three different businesses of his own there, and remains on retainer as a consultant for Boeing.) James C. Floyd, an outstanding aircraft designer and aerodynamicist, went back to practise his profession in England.

Immediately after the February 20th announcement, a number of American aircraft and aero-space firms sent recruiters to Toronto to attempt to contact and secure the services of senior Avro and Orenda personnel. Since there was nothing left for them in Canada in most cases, they inundated immigration authorities of the United States with business. Their skills were prized in the United States.

The Americans' National Aeronautical and Space Administration (NASA), which had just been formed from its predecessor organization, the National Advisory Committee for Aeronautics (NACA), was highly desirous of acquiring the services of leading Avro engineers. After trying vainly to find employment in Canada, Fred Matthews emigrated with about two dozen of his senior associates. These people were soon put to work on the manned space program.

They found the reaction of the knowledgeable NASA people most interesting. The NASA engineers, of course, knew a great deal about the *Arrow* and about its great power plant. NACA had been directly involved in the testing, having provided wind tunnel and other testing facilities at Langley Field and elsewhere for the *Arrow* project. Fred Matthews and his Avro associates were asked by several baffled NASA engineers why the Canadian government would cancel an outstanding aircraft like the *Arrow*. The NASA staff were simply incredulous at the Canadian government's cancelling what the NASA people called a "superlative engine", the Orenda *Iroquois*. Mr. Matthews' letters reflect his frustration at having had no rational answer.

One of the Avro engineers in the group with whom Matthews found himself was James A. Chamberlin, Chief Aerodynamicist for Avro Aircraft. If his qualifications were no longer of any great moment to the Canadian government, they were speedily recognized and exploited by the American government through NASA. Within a few months Chamberlin's ability was recognized, and he was appointed NASA's over-all manager for Project Gemini, in which post he had prime responsibility for the project's basic mission — which was to send two American astronauts on a 14 day orbit of the earth. It is perhaps sufficient commentary on the skills that the cancellation decision discarded to point out that, after being forced to leave Canada in the ranks of the unemployed, Chamberlin was soon in charge of an American government operation with a budget of 500 million dollars, and directing a staff comprising 160 engineers and technicians. (At a much later stage Chamberlin was sought out and hired by McDonnell-Douglas. Fred Matthews is presently in a senior position doing defence-related work for RCA in Massachusetts.)

The resulting cost to Canada of the brain drain effected by the *Arrow* cancellation is beyond calculation. If the handful of men located almost at random for the requisite background information for this account happen to constitute a representative sampling, Canada's loss was heavy indeed — a loss of leaders, of people with initiative and skill far above average. No country can afford to export people whose outstanding ability provides the intellectual capital sustaining jobs for scores or hundreds of others.

On the material side, the cost is more obvious. Our surviving aircraft industry in Canada is now in precarious health. It is perfectly clear that when Canadian plants are called upon to build

Left: *A spectacular shot of a night Bomarc launch.*
(BOEING)

The Diefenbaker government cancelled the Arrow program in 1959, ostensibly on the ground that new manned interceptors were not required, and that the sub-sonic CF-100s could fill the interceptor role satisfactorily in Canada. Just two years later, in 1961, the same government made arrangements with the United States to acquire supersonic F-101 Voodoos like the one shown below.

(A. SIEMENS)

Above: *A side view of CF-101 Voodoo 101028 of 425 Sqn. Bagotville, Quebec. Although Voodoos are now being phased out of even the Air National Guard in the United States, the Canadian Air Force has been reduced to such straits that its Voodoos will have to discharge their primary interceptor role — if they can be kept in the air that long — until 1983, when the aircraft to be acquired under Canada's New Fighter Program should be ready for squadron service.* (D. M. PEDEN)

Below: *Canadair built CF-104 Starfighter 104754 of 417 Squadron, Cold Lake, Alberta. Originally designed as a day interceptor, Canada purchased these aircraft for use in Europe in the strike-reconnaissance role.* (D. M. PEDEN)

Above: *After acquiring Voodoos and Starfighters in 1961 and 1962, the Canadian government began building Northrop F-5's under licence in 1965 at the Canadair plant in Quebec. CF-5D 116843 is from 419 Sqn. in Cold Lake, Alberta.*

(D. M. PEDEN)

Below: *A single seat CF-5, 116721. The government has announced its intention of relegating these to a purely training role once the 130-150 new aircraft are acquired under Canada's New Fighter Program.*

(D. M. PEDEN)

Grumman's F-14 Tomcat carries the world's most advanced air-to-air missile, the Phoenix. A computer controlled swing-wing and a highly sophisticated fire control system combine to make this aircraft the best air defence interceptor extant.

(G. L. MARSHAL)

and assemble components for whatever foreign-designed fighter our government next buys, they are going to be hard put to recruit the skilled tradesmen required — tradesmen we once had in such numbers that an estimated 30,000 were thrown out of work early in 1959. David Mundy, president of the Air Industries Association of Canada, was deploring as recently as April 10th, 1978, the significant shortage of skilled labour. Speaking at a seminar sponsored by the Association, he said bluntly: ". . . we lack skills in all areas of our operations, from the factory floor to management . . ." It will take a long time and a heavy capital expenditure to train men into these skills again. One of the economic factors lost sight of in February, 1959, was the value to the country of the asset represented by the skills Canada was about to throw away, and the serious results of the abandonment of the high level of research and development that were necessary concomitants of the whole *Arrow* program.

Some of those results are readily discernible in Canadian industry in 1978. At the beginning of June, 1978, the Science and Technology Ministry of Canada's federal government announced a major shift in Ottawa's purchasing policy. The announced objective was to double Canada's research and development effort over the next six years. The Minister, Mr. Judd Buchanan, pointed out that the research and development effort in Canada presently runs at only .9% of GNP, a figure which is well below the levels maintained in the United States and in other highly industrialized nations. It was pointed out that although the government buys four billion dollars worth of goods and services annually, only 1.3 billion is spent on high technology products such as electronics and data processing products. Those happen to be the very sort of products and services that were eliminated in 1958 with the cancellation of the ASTRA weapons and guidance systems. The *Arrow* and *Iroquois* programs themselves both involved a great deal of research and development; and that would undoubtedly have continued if the appropriate branches of the industry had not been scattered before the winds.

Other ramifications of the cancellation, to industry in Canada generally, were never understood by the government. When Avro and Orenda first started operations in Canada, the majority of the components they used, particularly in the case of Orenda, were high grade items and specialty items not manufactured locally. Avro raised standards in Canadian industry generally, and raised them significantly. Its suppliers were continually being pressed to up-grade their work and build to finer tolerances than they had hitherto attempted. The overall effects on a fairly broad spectrum of Canadian industry were highly beneficial, making them competitive in fields where they had always had to defer to foreign manufacturers. In its early days Orenda Engines Ltd. had to import the great majority of its basic components from the United States. In 1959 all but ten or 15 per cent of the components Orenda required were being built in Canada. But the greatest tragedy at Orenda, a tragedy for Canada, was what happened to the *Iroquois* engine.

It will be remembered that up to the time of cancellation of the *Arrow*, the costs of the *Iroquois* project had run to 87 million dollars. Regarding these costs, the company's projections had been phenomenally accurate. Back in November, 1956, it had estimated that the costs to this point would run to $85,707,548. After the cancellation the company estimated that to go on and complete the Official Type Test would run the costs to over $93,000,000 i.e., a further expenditure of approximately $7,000,000. Once work had been halted for any length of time this figure would quickly rise to $10,000,000 because of wide-ranging start-up costs.

Because of the circumstances, the size of the additional investment really left the company with Hobson's choice. Despite the great potential of the engine it was clearly hopeless to attempt to persuade Mr. Diefenbaker to reverse his decision. Thus the remaining alternatives were: to complete the Type Test at the company's own expense and look to the Curtiss-Wright and other foreign manufacturing royalties for recovery of its investment, to seek financial assistance from the U.S. government, or to abandon the entire project and swallow the loss.

Unfortunately, the United States government, which had been interested, and very helpful, in the early development of the

Iroquois, was definitely not desirous of seeing it produced by Curtiss-Wright. It had turned distinctly unenthusiastic when the Curtiss-Wright contract had been announced by Orenda.

In the early stages of development of the *Iroquois,* Orenda's management and engineers had developed a close liaison with the USAF and the Assistant Secretary of Air Force. The fruits of this liaison had been the wind tunnel test facilities and the B-47 aircraft — both provided free of charge.

As development of the *Iroquois* engine progressed further, Orenda was asked by the Americans to canvass the possibility of negotiating arrangements with any of three companies who might be interested in its manufacture. But the three companies named did not include Pratt & Whitney, Curtiss-Wright, or General Electric, the Big Three. Orenda's representatives could readily understand why Pratt & Whitney and General Electric were left out. Those companies already had big-engine programs, and were clearly not in need of further assistance from the American government. But this did not apply to Curtiss-Wright, a company that had sustained severe setbacks in development programs of moderate-sized engines. However, for whatever reasons, the USAF and the staff of the Assistant Secretary of the Air Force indicated that no further support would be given to Curtiss-Wright.

The Orenda management duly visited the three companies thus nominated, and initiated exploratory discussions on the question of manufacturing rights for the *Iroquois.* However, in each case the companies favoured by the American government wanted at least part of the compensation for the *Iroquois* licence rights to consist of a swap of their own engine designs — and these companies had only small-sized engines to offer, which were of no interest to Orenda.

Even Curtiss-Wright, when it came into the picture, offered rights to a small engine as part compensation. Orenda's vice-president, Charles Grinyer emphasized to Crawford Gordon that these had no value so far as Orenda was concerned. Furthermore, Grinyer was strongly opposed to entering into a contract with Curtiss-Wright in light of probable USAF reaction to a deal with that company. But from Crawford Gordon's point of view a contract with Curtiss-Wright had several factors in its favour.

Curtiss-Wright was a large and prestigious member of the American aero industry. "Their recent failures", Charles Grinyer pointed out, "were not known outside a small band of specialists. Curtiss-Wright had a strong lobby in Washington; so that, all in all, a deal with them might very well be the best possible. We did not expect the USAF to object so strongly; but they did. The door was closed on the *Iroquois*."

The loss of the prospects of assistance from the United States government virtually decided the issue as far as Crawford Gordon was concerned. At this point the company had already had to absorb $3,500,000 of its original investment. Additional costs and interest, not recoverable unless the Type Test was completed, brought Orenda's out-of-pocket to $6,000,000. For the company, on its own initiative and without some Canadian government assistance and goodwill, to pour in another $10,000,000 plus interest, and count on Curtiss-Wright to build enough *Iroquois* engines to return the entire investment to Orenda through licence payments, was a decision which was not defensible on the basis of business considerations.

So the great *Iroquois* engine died.

Most Canadians do not realize to this day what an asset was lost in the abandonment of the *Iroquois* engine when it was virtually ready to go through its Type Test. If one were to ask them, however, if they recalled how important a factor the famous Rolls Royce *Merlin* engines had been to Britain's survival in World War II, a large proportion would remember that fact. Most of them would remember that famous series of engines, and the aircraft they powered to victory: the *Spitfires, Hurricanes* and *Mustangs* of Fighter Command, and the *Lancasters, Halifaxes* and *Mosquitos* of Bomber Command. And yet, the Orenda *Iroquois* marked an even more substantial improvement over its immediate predecessors than had the great Rolls Royce *Merlins*.

Again, a comparison with today's technology, almost 20 years after the death of the *Iroquois*, brings home the tremendous achievement of Charles Grinyer and his Orenda engineers. The

Iroquois was designed to produce 25,000 pounds of thrust with afterburning. The latest Pratt & Whitney engine is the F100-PW-100, two of which power the F-15 *Eagle* and have given it a clutch of world's climbing records. That engine, Pratt & Whitney says, generates 25,000 pounds of thrust with afterburner augmentation.

To explain its power to laymen in terms they can understand more readily, its builders liken its output to the combined power of a line of 254 diesel locomotives. And yet the first models of the *Iroquois*, produced almost 20 years ago, were designed to turn out the same awesome power *then*. What would they have been capable of today if they had gone through an evolution of improved and refined models like the great *Merlin* series? What did Canadians throw away for the lack of an additional ten million dollar investment?

The Canadian government, which had already put $87,000,000 into the development of the engine, and had seen it progress to the point where it promised almost certainly to be far and away the best jet engine in the world, chose not to volunteer any further assistance of any type whatever. They stood back and watched while the Canadian taxpayers' investment — and an asset that could conceivably have played a vital role in NATO's security — vanished into thin air.

Another consequence of the *Arrow* cancellation was that for some time the conduct of the American government in the affair was the subject of considerable critical comment. But more than superficial analysis was required on this count; there were several factors to consider, and the American position was not devoid of merit.

It was quite true that the Americans had initially given moral support to Canada's developing a supersonic interceptor with the high performance spectrum ordained for the *Arrow*. The free use of American testing facilities, and the loan of the B-47 for the air testing of the *Iroquois*, were but the material manifestations of a strong ground swell of support for the Canadian venture. Behind the scenes there were even more promising trends. Recognizing that a program of this scale imposed a significant financial burden on the

Canadian economy, senior American officers had been sympathetic to the idea of the United States buying at least a small number of *Arrows* to help reduce unit cost. Air Marshal Slemon actually received assurances from the Chief of Staff USAF that purchases would be forthcoming. Such assurances were not binding, of course, and were understood not to be; but it appears that the matter had been cleared, at least tentatively, at the level of the U.S. Secretary.

Almost as soon as he had taken office as Prime Minister, Mr. Diefenbaker began undercutting the Canadian position by making extravagant statements regarding his government's intention to effect a realignment of Canadian trade, diverting it away from the United States. Blunt projections of a switch of 15 per cent of Canada's imports, from the U.S. to Britain, were not something the Americans could laugh off, not when they came from America's largest trading partner. Had Mr. Diefenbaker given some thought to the ammunition he was so generously handing to the lobby of the American aircraft industry, he would undoubtedly have been much more circumspect in his utterances. He appears not to have realized that, at least in George Pearkes' view, some American purchases of the *Arrow* were almost essential if the unit costs were going to be held within a readily acceptable range, and that by dampening the American ardor to purchase the *Arrow* he was inflating what he saw as his own economic problem regarding the National Defence budget.

In short order, in the corridors of power in the United States, enthusiasm for the both the *Arrow* and the Canadian Prime Minister began to wane. The Secretary of the Air Force in the U.S. did not have to have it explained to him that, with Prime Minister Diefenbaker talking about sharply reducing Canadian imports from the U.S., and making other speeches that were easy to construe as anti-American, the President would simply be courting embarrassment were he to send to Congress a Defence appropriation incorporating 200 or 300 million dollars for the purchase of Canadian aircraft.

As the Americans drew back, and George Pearkes had to return to Ottawa and report his inability to get a firm purchase order, Mr. Diefenbaker further diminished Canada's prospects of success by his press conference statements of September 23rd, 1958. Once he had thus publicly expressed reservations about the *Arrow,* and, indeed, about the future of all manned interceptors, the chances of selling it to other countries became infinitesimal. To state publicly that the *Arrow's* development program was being continued only "as a measure of insurance" was hardly a ringing endorsement of the aircraft or an affirmation of his own faith in it. The Americans had every justification, from that point on, for taking the position that if the Canadian government hadn't sufficient faith in the *Arrow* to put it into production — even limited production — how could *they,* the American government, possibly justify its purchase to their own electorate?

For Canada to go to outsiders and expect to interest them in *Arrows* after this public confession of doubt by the Prime Minister, was like the farmer lamenting to the visiting travelling salesman the ravages of an epidemic causing a high proportion of his poultry to drop dead from disease, then expecting the visitor to show enthusiasm over an invitation to stay for a dinner of chicken-à-la-king.

Approaching the U.K. authorities to sell the *Arrow* after September 23rd, 1958, must have made George Pearkes feel like W. S. Gilbert's rich attorney attempting to extol the virtues of his spinster daughter:

> "You'll soon get used to her looks," said he,
> "and a very nice girl you'll find her!
> "She may very well pass for forty-three
> in the dusk, with a light behind her!"[1]

Whether the Americans would have purchased *Arrows* had they been presented under different circumstances, by different people, is impossible to say.

If Canada had gone ahead with a production run of even 50 or 100 aircraft, the chances are that the superlative performance of the *Arrow* with the *Iroquois* engine would in due course, have opened the door for an American order, and perhaps for other

---

1. "Trial by Jury".

orders as well. Admittedly, an extraordinary performance would have been required; but there is every reason for believing that the performance of *Arrow* No. 6 and its successors would have been spectacular enough that the American government, with some discreet nudging from the NORAD commanders, would have found it easy to justify acquisition of the *Arrow*, at least pending the development of an American fighter with matching performance. In spite of the pressures of domestic politics, the American government had in fact established at least one precedent in 1951.

At the time of the war in Korea, the USAF had been looking for a high-speed aircraft to discharge the intruder and tactical bomber role. The British twin jet *Canberra* had a performance that met or exceeded all the American specifications and put that aircraft in a class by itself amongst the other competitors. The American government thereupon made the necessary arrangements for the *Canberra* to be built under licence in the United States (as the B-57), and on March 23rd, 1951, the Martin firm received an order to build 250 B-57As. Tactical Air Command received its first B-57s in June, 1954, and these "foreign imports" were still in active service at the time of the *Arrow* cancellation. Indeed some variants of the type are in service today.

Cynics would discount the evidentiary value of this incident and take a longer term view, pointing, with some justification, to the singular lack of success — and the in-fighting — attending attempts at arms standardization ever since the organization of NATO in 1949. The very limited successes included a 500 aircraft run of Fiat G.91s, shared between Germany and Italy, and the selection of the Breguet *Atlantic* in 1959 as a maritime patrol aircraft for NATO, of which it is estimated that approximately 60 would be required. Against these relatively small orders, critics would match the later successes for American-produced aircraft. In the early '60s the Lockheed F-104 *Starfighter* and the rights thereto were marketed very successfully to a number of NATO countries. Before 1968 some 950 F-104Gs had been produced — a nice bit of business for Lockheed.

The contemporary scene provides those sceptical of American

military altruism with further ammunition. It had been widely concluded that West Germany's highly efficient *Leopard II* tank would be the clear choice for standardization as the main battle tank of the NATO partners. But in 1977 the U.S. Army gave a $4.7 billion contract to Chrysler Corporation to build 3,325 tanks of its design, the XM-1[1]. Representative Les Aspin, a Democrat from Wisconsin, implied that the testers could see virtues in the Chrysler tank not discernible to him, alleging that the applicable reliability standards required the NATO tank to run an average of 320 miles without a major breakdown, whereas, he said, in tests conducted in the summer of 1977, the Chrysler XM-1 was breaking down every 100 miles while being tested under conditions that were so favourable as to be unrealistic. "A vehicle with 150 miles between failures", Aspin said, "would have less than a 50-50 chance of getting from army headquarters in West Germany to the nearest Warsaw Pact border without breaking down."

But current jockeying amongst the NATO partners is less relevant to the *Arrow's* story than the fact of the *Canberra* contract, and the generally sympathetic atmosphere for the *Arrow* that prevailed in high command circles in the United States. Had Canada proceeded to production with the Mark II *Arrow*, its performance promised to have been so improved over the Mark I's, and the *Starfighter's*, that Canada would have had every reasonable prospect of making foreign sales. It had done so with the *Arrow's* predecessor, the CF-100, although admittedly on a very small scale; and the performance of that product, and of Orenda engines generally, had given Avro Aircraft and Orenda Engines Ltd. widespread recognition. The public vacillation and timidity of the Canadian government in the autumn of 1958, prejudicial as they undoubtedly were to the *Arrow's* fate, could have been overcome by a winner's performance — and the *Arrow* had all the earmarks of a champion.

By killing it the government added to the earlier enumerated consequences of that decision one additional factor. They deprived

---

1. The Bonn government had to be satisfied with the U.S.'s agreement that the tank would be armed with the German-designed 120 mm. gun, produced in New York, under licence from Kraus Maffei, at the Army's Watervliet arsenal.

the Canadian people of a great and potentially important psychological stimulus. Geographic and cultural factors have given Canadians an uphill battle to win in their struggle for unity and a national identity. Their fighting services' successes have elevated and consolidated the country's spirit and self-respect during and immediately after two world wars, and to a lesser extent after the war in Korea. To have won the palm unequivocally as the leader of the western world in the high technology field of military aircraft design would have been a significant event in the development of national consciousness and identity. Prime Minister Diefenbaker's reference to the "sense of pride of achievement" indicated that he had caught a glimpse of this nebulous potential in passing, but he never saw it clearly, and he greatly underrated its importance. Perhaps to him it was just a case of winning a world's speed record, a temporary fillip to national vanity.

How unfortunate for the whole country that his advisers had not been able to imbue him with an enthusiasm for the continuation and expansion of Canada's already impressive role in aircraft development and utilization. He could not help but be aware that Canadians had long been among the most progressive and innovative in the use and development of aircraft. With his powerful oratorical talents the Prime Minister had been able, during his latest election campaign, to excite and marshal national sentiment behind him for something as intangible as his great "vision" of northern development. What his talents could have achieved for the development and exploitation of Canada's lead in the high technology aircraft and electronics industries can only be imagined; but if his interest could have been captured, and had he been fired with enthusiasm for the expansion of this new industrial frontier, the story of the ensuing years could have been vastly different.

Instead, the Prime Minister never acquired any feel for the possibilities of the highly competitive and rapidly advancing aero-space industry. The homespun parallel he drew — in his March 3rd, 1959, speech — between the alleged redundancy of a supersonic interceptor and a change in agricultural technology with which he was familiar, showed little evidence of empathy. Rather, the Prime Minister sounded, uncharacteristically, like a throwback to some bucolic bumpkin of a previous era. "There is no purpose in manufacturing horse collars when horses no longer exist . . .", he said. As he was saying this, Vladimir Myasishchev, the designer of the latest Russian bomber, the *Bounder*, was readying the first prototype of that aircraft for the flight trials it actually began in September, 1959[1].

Without any really knowledgeable interest in aircraft development, the Prime Minister never acquired any enthusiasm for the *Arrow*. On the contrary, he took an increasingly jaundiced view of the whole operation. As difficulties seemed to him to be mounting, and costs climbing, he took counsel of his fears, rejected the clear and unequivocal views of his Chief of Air Staff, and rationalized his way into an uninspiring "let's cut our losses" type of approach. Apart from the increased risk to which that approach could have exposed Canada, it also cost the country more than can yet be calculated, pushing Canadians back into a colonial position in a field in which briefly they had led the world, and sapping national confidence instead of bolstering it. A leader with a little more "damn the torpedoes" determination could have injected new and fully justified pride into all Canadians, and could have reinforced and consolidated the success of a most promising industrial bridgehead into the new territory of high technology supersonic aircraft design.

Instead, the *Arrow* and the *Iroquois* were given their quietus. The evidence of the *Arrow's* surpassing technological superiority was destroyed by torch with a thoroughness that seemed to bespeak vindictiveness or guilt, and attention was diverted from the whole affair as soon as the noisy but half-hearted recriminations of the opposition had been walled off with a firebreak of meretricious "new strategy" that flew in the face of the opinions voiced by leading professional airmen in both Canada and the United States.

---

1. Myasishchev had begun his design around 1955, and his hope had been to turn out a bomber with a high payload and a cruising speed approximately 50 per cent better than any bomber then in the air. Had he been wholly successful, highly supersonic interceptors would have been required, urgently, to meet the threat. As it happened, the *Bounder* did set a number of payload-to-height records, but the first versions fell well short of Myasishchev's ambitious speed objectives.

The *Bomarcs*, which the Prime Minister had turned to as a bargain basement panacea for the problems of aerial defence, became an albatross around his government's neck. Persuaded by well-meaning idealists in his cabinet, men like Howard Green, that Canada should adopt a non-nuclear stance and set an example to the world, Mr. Diefenbaker balked at installing nuclear warheads on the weapons, despite what he had said and clearly implied in his *Arrow* cancellation speech. Somehow the Howard Green contingent seemed to suggest that, with Canada parading about the international scene purer than the driven snow, i.e., carrying only common, garden variety bombs and cannons for killing purposes instead of even deadlier weapons, potentially aggressive middle-powers would recognize their turpitude and hastily forswear anything more damaging than slingshots in their military inventories. The super-powers, too, would be shamed by Canada's virtue, and peace, perfect peace, would descend upon the globe, almost before we could beat the cradles of our non-nuclear *Bomarcs* into bridge girders.

Lester Pearson, whose Liberal party had been energetically disseminating the same non-proliferation line, neatly reversed his field on the issue, undertook to accept the nuclear warheads — as a temporary expedient only, of course — and after being nosed out in the 1962 election, won the 1963 election almost by default, as the Diefenbaker cabinet disintegrated in internecine strife.

By 1963 the "new strategy" of the *Arrow's* opponents had, of necessity, been modified out of recognition. The Diefenbaker government itself had no sooner killed the *Arrow*, pooh-poohing the need for new supersonic interceptors, than it set about acquiring, in 1961, 66 supersonic F-101 *Voodoo* interceptors built by McDonnell-Douglas in the United States. There was little stress laid on the fact that the *Voodoo* was rated at Mach 1.85, as compared with the Mach 2.5 anticipated for the Mark II *Arrow*. Shortly thereafter, Canada purchased 30 or 40 training-version *Starfighters* (F-104Cs) from Lockheed, and subsequently paid the necessary licence royalties to build 110 of the F-104G version at the Quebec plant of Canadair. Still later, Canadair built a larger number of the strike-reconnaissance version of the *Starfighter*. These aircraft,

McDonnell-Douglas F-15 Eagle. The Eagle and Tomcat are the most capable of the New Fighter Aircraft candidates, their only drawback being their heavy price tags. The Eagle holds a clutch of world climbing records and is undoubtedly one of the best fighter aircraft in service anywhere. The Canadian roundel on '058, above, was applied at CFB Trenton, September 1978.

(G. L. MARSHAL)

Above: *The Panavia Tornado, built by a consortium backed by the governments of Britain, West Germany and Italy. The Tornado is probably unsurpassed for low level navigational avionics.* (BRITISH AIRCRAFT CORPORATION)

Below: *General Dynamics' F-16, a single-seat, single-engined light weight fighter of exceptional performance.* (GENERAL DYNAMICS)

Above: *The Northrop F-18-L competes in Canadian markings. Northrop is marketing this aircraft aggressively, and hopes that its price will give it the edge in the Canadian Fighter competition.* (NORTHROP)

Below: *The first prototype of the Mirage 2000. Dassault-Breguet, the manufacturer, withdrew this aircraft from the Canadian competition at the end of February, 1978.* (AMD-BA)

Above: *This is all that could be hidden from the torch squad sent to destroy the Arrows: Arrow No. 6 was fitted with Iroquois engines, the first Arrow equipped with that great power plant, and was due to fly in March, 1959. Prime Minister Diefenbaker cancelled the whole program on February 20th, 1959. This nose section is what Canadians have to show for the hundreds of millions of dollars expended on the development program.* (PHOTO BY A. B. PEDEN)

Below: *The last vestiges of P.S. 13 — an Iroquois engine on display at the National Aeronautical Collection at Rockcliffe in Ottawa.* (A. J. SHORTT)

inferior in performance to the *Arrow*, were built primarily for the strike role of Canada's NATO Air Division in Europe — a role for which the *Arrow* could readily have been modified.

After taking office in 1963, the Pearson government did not wait long to demonstrate that in this field they could at least match the Conservatives in foolishness. Early in its turbulent career the Pearson government made large expenditures to build, under licence, both the single and two-seat versions of Northrop's F-5 *Freedom Fighter* — again at Canadair's Quebec plant.

The F-5 was specifically designed to be a very low cost, lightweight fighter. Bearing that in mind, one certainly cannot fault Northrop for the fact that its performance, compared with the capabilities of heavier, more expensive fighters, is extremely limited. The engines of the F-5A turn up 4,080 pounds of thrust with afterburner augmentation. The *Iroquois* produced 25,000 pounds. The F-5A's maximum speed is quoted at Mach 1.43, some 700 m.p.h. slower than the projected speed of the Mark II *Arrow*. (At the beginning of February, 1978, when President Sadat was apprised of the fact that the United States was prepared to meet his request for modern new fighters by allowing Egypt to purchase 60 of the latest model *Freedom Fighter*, the F-5Es, he dismissed them contemptuously as "tenth rate".)

On these various models of inferior aircraft Canadian governments have spent hundreds of millions of dollars, after having killed a Canadian-designed interceptor that would have outperformed any of them.

Under Prime Minister Pearson, the *Bomarcs* were armed with nuclear warheads only briefly — then disarmed. Competing missile technology quickly rendered them obsolete. On the other hand, the logic of events has maintained the vital importance of the manned interceptor, and the latest indications in the murky world of military intelligence are that the importance of the manned interceptor is about to be emphatically underlined.

On June 19th, 1978, the Defence Intelligence Agency of the American government announced publicly, after lengthy closed-door testimony before the U.S. Senate's Armed Services Committee in

March, that the Soviets are developing a new nuclear bomber with performance characteristics very similar to those of the highly advanced American B-1 (which President Carter cancelled in 1977, against the advice of many professionals in the U.S. Defence Department.) Intelligence estimates are that the new Russian bomber will be operational in the early 1980's.

Looking back over the two decades, there is an old lesson to be re-learned in Canada from the sorry epilogue of the *Arrow*. National security cannot be procured on the cheap. Political leaders in democratic countries have always tended to shy away from that unpalatable truth. And yet, how many times in recent history have those same politicians, who shrank from asking the electorate to spend money on national security, unhesitatingly and shamelessly asked the country's youth to lay down their lives to restore it? A nation that cannot afford to build the best weapons for its defence forces, but which can afford to spend upwards of a billion and a half dollars for the sports spectacle of the Olympic Games, is in more serious trouble than its political leaders appear to realize.

Another lesson that Canada will have to re-learn, apparently, is that sophisticated defence industries cannot be erected overnight. When war and mortal danger become imminent, it is too late to set about trying to assemble an aircraft industry, or tank and gun factories, or shipyards. There is a price for keeping these facilities in existence in the piping times of peace. Countries which are not prepared to pay that price will ultimately pay a far higher one.

Chronological Table of Events

Acknowledgements

The author wishes to acknowledge, with sincere thanks, the assistance so generously given him by a number of people, many of whom corresponded with him at length answering questions, and culled their files for photographs, technical material, articles and notes — or granted interviews. A few names I have intentionally omitted, only because erroneous inferences might be drawn as to the facts each gave me. I express my gratitude to:

John H. Newland — Manager - Public Relations, Boeing Commercial
Airplane Company, Seattle.
Norman Malayney — Western Canada Aviation Museum, Winnipeg.
Fred C. Matthews — Lexington, Massachusetts.
Charles A. Grinyer — Caledon, Ontario.
R. W. Bradford — Curator, Aviation and Space Division, The National
Museum of Science and Technology, Ottawa.
A. J. Shortt — Assistant Curator, Aviation and Space Division,
The National Museum of Science and Technology, Ottawa.
Major-General (retired) M. T. Friedl — Ottawa.
Honourable Barnett Danson — Minister of National Defence, Ottawa.
Colonel J. G. Boulet — Director of Information Services, National
Defence Headquarters, Ottawa.
Commanding Officer — Canadian Forces Photographic Unit, CFB Ottawa.
Air Vice-Marshal (retired) John Easton — Ottawa.
Harry C. Ralph — Kirkland, Washington.
Carl V. Lindow — Redmond, Washington.
Edward J. Silling — Kent, Washington.
Carl Vincent — Stittsville, Ontario.
Honourable John Stetson — Secretary of the Air Force, Washington, D.C.
Peter J. Brennan — Ottawa.

NOTE: Many of the technical and design details of the *Arrow* given in this book are based on material drawn from a variety of sources: (1) A.V. Roe (Canada) Ltd. material now in the archives of the Air and Space Division of the National Museum of Science and Technology at Ottawa; (2) the definitive paper entitled "The Canadian Approach to All-Weather Interceptor Development" presented by Mr. J. C. Floyd before the Royal Aeronautical Society in London on October 9th, 1958, and recorded in the December, 1958 issue of the Journal of the Royal Aeronautical Society (Vol. 62, No. 576); (3) a large number of articles in then current issues of such magazines as "Aircraft", "Canadian Aviation" and "Avro Newsmagazine".

APPENDIX I

The magnitude of the PS 13 project and the relatively advanced status of the *Arrow* aircraft program prompted serious consideration of what would be the best Engineering Organization to ensure success. Prior to the PS 13 project, and from the time when Orenda Ltd. had its early beginnings as 'Turbo Research', a very capable design engineering team had been established with experience gained from the 'Chinook' engine and from the early units of the Orenda series of engines. This team had been under the direction of Paul Dilworth as Chief Engineer, and Winnet Boyd as Chief Design Engineer. In early 1952, Val Cronstedt, an engineer from Pratt & Whitney, became Vice-President of Engineering, and it was from this time onwards that serious thoughts on future engines received much attention, leading to PS 13.

It was realized at the outset that the new organization must be able to deal with the specializations involved and would have to have full authority over all matters from the design concept through to procurement, manufacture, assembly, test and disassembly of the engines — everything right through to a successful Type Test. This was not achieved in one step; but very quickly an organization was established which gave confidence to the company, to Avro Canada, and to the various government departments involved with the *Arrow* program.

The following chart shows the basic arrangement of the senior divisions of the Engineering Department of Orenda Ltd.

ORENDA ENGINEERING ORGANIZATION CHART

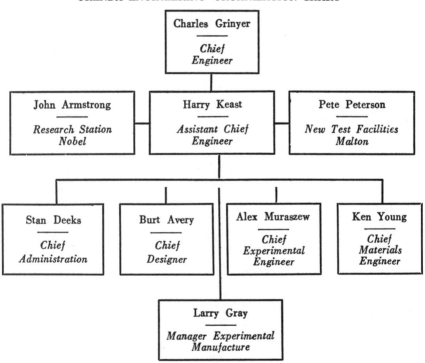

At the peak of the program there were about 1,650 people involved at Orenda; about half of these were on the Engineering payroll; the other half were involved in procurement, manufacture, and assembly of experimental components and engines. There were about 320 professional engineers engaged on this work, of whom about half were Canadians. The other half came from such countries as France, Holland, Poland, Sweden, and Great Britain.

In addition to the senior people named on the organization chart, there were 1,650 people engaged on the program all of whom, at one time or another, played important roles in the success of the program. Help was also obtained from the production side of the company and the Service Department, so that almost every employee may have been involved at some time. In trying to acknowledge this involvement, Charles Grinyer has suggested that we print the names of the last list of the members joining the company's "Ten-Year Club." Even this amounts to only a small fraction of those involved. Nevertheless, the publication of these names indicates that the success was due to more than just a few senior people.

1958 ADDITION TO ORENDA
TEN-YEAR CLUB

Carl Allen
Don Anderson
Floyd Archer
Bob Armour
John Armstrong
Phil Ayers

Al Bain
Harry Ballantyne
Jimmie Beedman
Ben Benbow
Gerry Benoy
Charlie Birch
Jimmie Blair
Frank Blanchard
Al Bodiam
Curly Bolton
Albert Bown
Bob Boyd
Bill Boyd
Al Breadman
Herb Brook
Browne Brownie
Gene Bryans
Bob Burrel
Ross Burton

Ralph Cameron
Jack Carroll
Art Chapman
George Chettle
George Chippendale
Dave Chirnside
Jack Clarke
Ken Colby
Peter Comery
Charlie Cooper
Jimmy Cooper
Earl Copeland
Al Craig
Bob Curtis

Jim Davidson
Bette DeJersey
George Dewsnap
Art Dibben
Bill Duncan
Jeff Durrant
Ken Dutton

Eric Early
Claire Eatock
Tob Ebbern
Andy Edward
Ted Elder
Teddy Evans

Fab Fabierkiewicz
George Faichine
Gene Farion
Ross Ferguson
Red Findlay
Rene Fleming
Les Foster
Albert Frisby
Ed Gale

Blanche Gallagher
Chester Giles
John Gilmour
Al Golightley
Jack Gomm
Eddie Gougeon
Gordon Graham
Bill Graydon
Clarence Griffith

Curly Hall
Ken Harding
Stan Harding
Ivan Harris
Ken Haw
Clair Hawn
Bill Heraldson
George Hillman
Jim Hillson
Ron Hiorns
Norm Horn
Andy Horsman
Joe Hubble
Bill Humenick
Garnet Hunter
Fred Hussey
Hutch Hutchson

Art Inscoe

Ken James
Fred Jarman
Jerry Jerome
Reg Jones

Gord Kearns
Gordy Kearns
Gord Keeler
Bill Kemp
Dan Kingston
Bruce Kirby
Harold Kochler

Gord Lamb
Gil Larner
Joe Lewin
George Lindsay
Dave Lucier
Doug Ludlow
Bill Lunt

Audry MacDonald
Sam Martins
Ed McCluskey
(Mrs.) McGinnis
(Mrs.) McGrath
Ken McGuire
Archie McIntyre
Norm McLaughlin
George McLean
Frank McShane
Mac McVetty
Don Morrison
Howard Mulliss
Bob Mushet
Jack Nesbitt
Wait Newbold

Karl O'Conner
Oke Okie

Bill Palmer
Bob Pausey
Lus Penrose
Herb Perks
Bill Pinder
Chuck Pover
Ed Pullen

Walter Reid
Less Ridley
Al Robb
(Mrs.) Robertson
Reg Rodgers
Jerry Russ
Jimmy Russel

Bob Sachs
Reg Sampson
Jack Savage
Bill Scarr
Clarence Scott
Russ Selway
Gord Shaw
Reg Simpson
Aubrey Smith
George Smith
Murray Snider
Al Spier
Alfy Stevenson
Frank Strugnell
Ralph Stucker
Art Sutton
Jack Swift
Charlie Sykes

Ed Taylor
Jerry Taylor
Harry Terrance
Fred Thomas
Tommy Thomas
Andy Thomson
Lloyd Thomson
Roy Trimble

Cec Vella
Tom Virkus

Dave Wales
Bill Walsh
Duffy Walsh
George Ward
Cliff Warren
Leo Watson
Sam Weller
Bill Williams
Aubrey White
Pete Willson
Len Wilson
Monty Woolley
Lefty Wright

Alf Yates

ADDENDUM

Fall of an Arrow was first published almost a decade ago. While comparisons and facts are somewhat dated, their application remains accurate. Minor additions and corrections are listed below.

Page	Line	
68	20	In 1984, Prime Minister Mulroney's Conservatives
137	3	won 211 seats out of 282.
69	9	"Somers" should read "Summers"
124	8	The Canadian government made the decision to purchase 138 F-18 Hornets, manufactured by the American firm McDonnell-Douglas, a variant of Northrop's F-18. (See photo page 179)
130	21	"contact" should read "contract"
135	10	Five years after the writing of the book, on August 31, 1983, another Korean Airlines aircraft, this time a "Jumbo" Boeing 747, flew into Russian airspace and was in fact intercepted by a Russian fighter and deliberately shot down. All 269 people aboard were killed.
155	7-8	Israel Aircraft Industries Ltd. is now called Israel Aviation Industries.
155	16	The cost of the updated "Lavi" fighter is projected at $34.5 million per aircraft. Israel is continuing to develop the fighter and as of June 30, 1986, as reported in *Forbes* magazine, had a prototype virtually ready to fly.

PHOTOGRAPH CREDITS

Photographs credited to Air and Space Division, National Museum, Ottawa, should now be credited to the National Aviation Museum.

Page 137, The Right Honourable John G. Diefenbaker/Photo by Duncan Cameron, Public Archives of Canada (PA-57930)